WASSERSTROM

D1554336

The Aquinas Lecture, 2002

ESCHATOLOGICAL THEMES IN MEDIEVAL JEWISH PHILOSOPHY

ARTHUR HYMAN

Under the auspices of the
Wisconsin-Alpha Chapter of Phi Sigma Tau

MARQUETTE
UNIVERSITY

PRESS

Library of Congress Cataloging-in-Publication Data

Hyman, Arthur, 1921-
  Eschatological themes in medieval Jewish philosophy / by
  Arthur Hyman.
     p. cm. — (The Aquinas lecture ; 2002)
Includes bibliographical references.
  ISBN 0-87462-169-0
  1. Eschatology, Jewish. 2. Philosophy, Jewish.
  3. Philosophy, Medieval. I. Title. II. Series.
B757.E72 H96 2002
181'.06—dc21

                                    2001008624

© 2002 Marquette University Press
Printed in the United States of America

MARQUETTE UNIVERSITY PRESS
MILWAUKEE

The Association of Jesuit University Presses

Prefatory

The Wisconsin-Alpha Chapter of Phi Sigma Tau, the International Honor Society for Philosophy at Marquette University, each year invites a scholar to deliver a lecture in honor of St. Thomas Aquinas.

The 2002 Aquinas Lecture, *Eschatological Themes in Medieval Jewish Philosophy*, was delivered on Sunday, February 24, 2002, by Arthur Hyman, Dean of the Bernard Revel Graduate School and Distinguished Service Professor of Philosophy at Yeshiva University. Previously Professor Hyman had been University Professor of Philosophy at Yeshiva University from 1972 to 1991, Professor of Philosophy from 1967 to 1972, and Associate Professor from 1961 to 1967. Prior to coming to Yeshiva, Professor Hyman had taught at Dropsie University and at the Jewish Theological Seminary. He received an M.H.L. from the Jewish Theological Seminary of America in 1955, a Ph.D. in 1953 and an M.A. in 1947 from Harvard University, and a B.A. from St. John's College, Maryland, in 1944.

He has been Visiting Professor of Jewish Philosophy at Hebrew University, Jerusalem, in 1969-1970, and at Bar Ilan University, Ramat Gan, in the summer of 1970. He has also been Visiting Professor of Philosophy at Columbia University, the University of California, San Diego, Yale University, and The Catholic University of America, as well as the Lady Davis Visiting Professor at Hebrew University.

Professor Hyman has received honorary degrees from Hebrew Union College-Jewish Institute of

Religion in 1994 and from the Jewish Theological
Seminary of America in 1987. He received the Award
for Textual Studies from the National Foundation
for Jewish Culture in 1999. He has served on the
executive committee and as president of the Society
for Medieval and Renaissance Philosophy. He was
elected a fellow of the American Academy for Jewish
Research in 1968 and served as its president from
1992 to 1996.

Professor Hyman's publications include four
volumes of *Maimonidean Studies*, which he edited,
a critical edition of the Hebrew text and an English
translation of *Averroes' De Substantia Orbis*, and
Essays in Medieval Jewish and Islamic Philosophy,
which he edited while contributing an essay. He
has also edited with others the *Salo W. Baron Jubilee
Volume* and the *Harry A. Wolfson Jubilee Volume*
and coauthored *Philosophy in the Middle Ages: The
Christian, Islamic, and Jewish Traditions*. Among
the most recent of his thirty some articles there
are: "Maimonide, partisan du libre arbitre ou
déterministe?" in *Actes du Colloque Maïmonide*,
"Averroes' Theory of the Intellect and the Ancient
Commentators," in *Averroes and the Aristotelian
Tradition*, "Spinoza on Possibility and Contingency,"
in *Meetings of the Minds: The Relations between
Medieval and Classical Modern European Philosophy*,
and "Medieval Jewish Philosophy as Philosophy, as
Exegesis, and as Polemic," in *Miscellanea Mediae-
valia*.

To Professor Hyman's distinguished list of
publications, Phi Sigma Tau is pleased to add:
Eschatological Themes in Medieval Jewish Philosophy.

Eschatological Themes in Medieval Jewish Philosophy

Introduction

This volume, written on the occasion of the Aquinas lecture at Marquette University, had a twofold origin. Having taught history of philosophy and, especially, the history of Jewish philosophy for a number of years, I became intrigued by problems of eschatology—problems which lie at the borderline of philosophy and Jewish tradition. This interest grew so much so, that I decided to offer a course on "Jewish Eschatology" as one of my graduate offerings at Yeshiva University. This course I have now given regularly over a number of years. A second interest which motivated this volume was an interest in Aristotle's psychological theories and their interpretation by the Hellenistic commentators, Alexander of Aphrodisias and Themistius, and the Muslim commentators, Avicenna and, especially, Averroes. It was the theories of these commentators that influenced the conceptions of the afterlife

which were formulated by those philosophers who
were followers of Aristotelian philosophy.

More immediately this volume was occasioned
by a discussion which appeared at the end of Rabbi
Moses ben Naḥman's (1194-1270), or Naḥmanides'
The Chapter on Reward (*sha' ar ha-gemul*), which
forms part of a larger work known as *Torat ha-
Adam*. In the larger work Naḥmanides deals with
matters pertaining to sickness, death, burial, and
mourning customs, but in the *Chapter on Reward*
he deals at length with matters of eschatology. He
presents and criticizes the opinions of Ibn Gabirol
and Maimonides (though he shows great respect for
the latter) and then presents his own opinion and
mentions approvingly the opinion of a predecessor,
Saadiah Gaon. As Naḥmanides sees it there are two
divergent opinions concerning eschatological topics.
There are the opinions of those whose theories are
based on philosophic psychology and then there are
the opinions of those who consider eschatology as a
continuation of history in some fashion. In addition,
these varying theories emphasize different aspects
of eschatology. While those who base themselves on
philosophical psychology are primarily interested
in the ultimate state of the intellect, which they
identify with immortality, those who see the fate of
the soul after death as part of a historical process are
more interested in the resurrection of the dead and
the state of the soul immediately after death.

The Naḥmanides passage that motivated this
volume reads as follows:

Truthfully [speaking], you will find in the philosophic works and prayers of some of the Spanish Sages that they do agree with [Maimonides'] opinion that '*olam ha-ba*' (the World to Come) is the World of Souls (Intellects). Thus, Rabbi Solomon ibn Gabirol (the Avicebron of the Latins) of blessed memory says in his prayer: "Under the Throne of Thy Glory, Thou hast established a resting place for the souls of Thy saints, and there is delight without end or limit, for it is the World to Come." Similarly, he prays, "And when Thou shalt take me out of this world, bring me in peace to the World to Come." However, you should accept our opinion, because we have spoken according to tradition (*ke-halakhah*) and have brought proof to our words from those of our Rabbis of blessed memory. I have found further that in his commentary on the Book of Daniel, the Gaon Rabbi Saadiah of blessed memory speaks of the meaning of the term "World to Come" in accordance with our words…. All, however, agree about the resurrection of the dead and the existence of that time in its general outlines and details…. The only [dissenting] opinion is that of Rabbi Moses [ben Maimon] of blessed memory who assigned a limited time to the resurrection (of the dead) after which everything returns to the World of Souls (Intellects)…. We, however, declare that the people of the resurrection will exist forever, from the time of the resurrection

of the dead to the World to Come, which is
an everlasting world.[1]

The history of eschatology in Jewish tradition
is varied and complex, and of it we can discuss
only one aspect—eschatology in medieval Jewish
philosophy. Besides its history in medieval Jewish
philosophy, eschatology found its place in the
bible, in the apocalyptic literature, in the variety
of rabbinic discussions, in prayers and liturgical
poems, in mysticism, in a secular (political) form
in modern literature, and in the controversies
between the orthodox and liberal movements in
modern times. In addition to all these, the history
of messianic pretenders and messianic movements
accompanied Jewish history throughout all of its
period until our own day. These also need to be
studied if one wants to present a full picture of
Jewish eschatology.[2]

Eschatological discussions are rather sparse in
the bible and they are not systematic. One hears
of *she'ol*, the nether-world, which is the abode of
the dead, and, while the rabbis find allusions to the
resurrection of the dead in the early books of the
bible, resurrection is not mentioned explicitly in
the canon until the book of Daniel. Perhaps the
most explicit biblical eschatological theme is that
of the Messiah. While it appears that the advent of
the Messiah, a descendant of the house of David
who was to reestablish the Davidic dynasty, was
originally expected still in biblical times, when the
Messiah did not appear, belief in him became a
part of eschatological speculations. Side by side

with descriptions of a personal Messiah, the bible
also describes messianic times. These are to be
times marked by the return of the Jewish people
to its land, times of peace and tranquillity for all
mankind, and times when all mankind will believe
in the one God and worship him.

In addition to the three major eschatological
themes—*she'ol*, Messiah and messianic times, and the
resurrection of the dead—the bible contained other
themes that were incorporated in eschatological
theories when these became more systematized. One
such is the War of Gog and Magog, the cataclysmic
war that is to precede the advent of the Messiah.
According to another theme, the advent of the
Messiah is to be announced by the prophet Elijah.
According to still another, the Messiah descendant of
David will be preceded by a Messiah descendant of
Joseph, a theory extracted from verses in the Books
of Obadiah and Zechariah. The Garden of Eden,
well known from the creation story, in a changed
form, also became part of the eschatological picture,
and so did the biblical *Gehinnom*, Hell.

Eschatological theories became more systematic
during the times of the rabbinic Sages. The
terminology now became fixed, but there were
variations in particulars. While the resurrection of
the dead was still a center piece of eschatological
speculations, one now hears of a final stage known
as the World to Come (*'olam ha-ba*) which takes
the place of the biblical *she'ol*. In a striking Mishnah
(legal text), one hears that all Israelites have a
share in the World to Come, but that those who
deny the resurrection of the dead will not have a

part in that World. From this Mishnah and other rabbinic sources it follows that the early rabbinic Sages made a determined effort to make a belief in the resurrection of the dead a required belief, particularly since it was denied by the Sadducees. The divergence of eschatological beliefs emerges from a description of the banquet that will be held at the end of time. According to some Sages, the flesh of the Behemot and Leviathan, monsters described in the book of Job, will be served at that banquet, while according to others the banquet will be more spiritual. According to these there will be neither eating nor drinking nor any other physical activity, but the righteous will sit with their crowns on their head and will enjoy the radiance of the divine presence.

In general, the sequence of eschatological events mentioned in the rabbinic literature may be described in the following fashion. Prior to the coming of the Messiah, a descendant of the House of David, there will be the War of Gog and Magog and during that time there will arise the Messiah son of Joseph. This Messiah will be killed and then Elijah will appear to announce the coming of Messiah son of David. During the time of the davidic Messiah, the dead will be resurrected and they will be judged. In continuity with messianic times there will arrive the World to Come in which, for most of the rabbinic Sages, the resurrected soul and body of those who are to be rewarded will continue to exist forever. This will also be the time when the wicked will be punished.

This brings us to the immediate topic of this volume, eschatological themes in the writings of the medieval Jewish philosophers. As is to be expected, such speculations became still more systematic, and philosophers attempted to provide philosophic explanations of eschatological themes wherever this was possible. In turn these attempts depended on different conceptions of what was possible for human reason, which, in turn, depended on a given philosopher's philosophic orientation.

The five thinkers represented here present five different approaches to matters of eschatology. Saadiah Gaon represents Muʿtazilite Kalâm, a movement that undertook to explain Scriptural difficulties and apparent contradictions by means of philosophic arguments. Since the Kalâm thinkers were more interested in resolving Scriptural problems than in establishing a systematic philosophy, their philosophic speculations were eclectic. Solomon Ibn Gabirol represents Neo-Platonism. As a Neo-Platonist he was primarily interested in the ultimate fate of the human soul. According to his opinion, the soul and, with it, the intellect came from the upper world, were joined to the human body, and in the end returned to the world from which they came. With Moses Maimonides we turn to the Aristotelians and their eschatological theories. As the Neo-Platonists they held that the World to Come consists of incorporeal intelligences. But the Aristotelians argued their case on the basis of Aristotle and his Hellenistic and Muslim commentators. Maimonides followed Alexander of Aphrodisias who held that the intellect starts out as a corporeal predisposition, but can in the end become incorporeal. For Gersonides, Averroes was the main interpreter. While Gersonides carefully reviews the opinions of various Aristotelian commentators, in the end he develops a theory of his own. For Gersonides, it is the individual acquired intellect which is immortal. A fifth opinion is represented by Naḥmanides who, on the whole, follows the opinion of the rabbinic Sages, even though philosophic arguments are not lacking from his exposition.

I wish to thank Professor John D. Jones, chair, and the members of the philosophy department of Marquette University for inviting me to give the Aquinas lecture. I feel greatly honored that they saw fit to include me among the distinguished scholars who have given these lectures in the past. I also want to thank the administration and my colleagues at Yeshiva University for providing me, over the years, with a hospitable home for my teaching and research. But most of all I wish to thank my wife, Batyah, for her patience and encouragement which made this volume possible.

Biblical and Rabbinic Antecedents

One of the striking features of the theology of the Hebrew Bible is how little space is devoted to eschatological speculations.[3] To be sure, one hears about *she'ol*, the abode of the dead, and about the Messiah, but, on the whole, these discussions are rather sketchy. In the canonical text the resurrection of the dead does not occur until the book of Daniel, and even there it is rather enigmatic, and the understanding of the text depends on interpretation. As we know from Josephus and Christian Scripture, the resurrection of the dead was subject to disagreement among Jewish sects. Before we then turn to the discussion and systematization of eschatological themes in medieval Jewish philosophy, we must take up briefly biblical and rabbinic antecedents.

As has already been noted, the primary biblical term for the afterlife is *she'ol*, a subterranean netherworld in which the dead exist as shades in physical form. In Psalm 18:6, for example, David describes his distress upon being pursued by Saul as "The cords of the nether-world (*she'ol*) surrounded me; the snares of death confronted me." Or again, we read in Psalm 116:3: "the cords of death compassed me, and the straits of the nether-world (*she'ol*) got hold upon me; I found trouble and sorrow." It also appears from Scriptures that God can save a person from *she'ol*, though it is never spelled out in what the salvation consists. Psalm 30:4 reads: "O Lord, Thou broughtest up my soul from the nether-world (*she'ol*); Thou didst keep me alive, so that I should not go down to the pit." And contrasting foolish people and the wise, Psalm 49:15-16 states: "Like sheep they [the foolish people] are appointed for the nether-world (*she'ol*).... But God will redeem my soul from the power of the nether-world (*she'ol*); for He shall receive me."

In most biblical passages it is assumed that the reader knows what *she'ol* is, but one receives a more explicit description in 1 Samuel, chap. 28:3-19. Saul, the first Israelite king, had prohibited divination by means of ghosts and familiar spirits. But when the

Philistines marched against him, Saul was afraid and
he inquired of the Lord what the future would hold.
When he received no answer in dreams, through
the Urim and Tumim, or through a prophet, he
turned to the very means he had prohibited. He
asked his servants to find him someone who could
predict the future by consulting with ghosts, the
very practice he had forbidden. They found him an
unnamed woman in Endor. Saul disguised himself
and when he came to the woman she at first refused
to practice what he had prohibited. When Saul
assured her of her safety, she brought up "an old
man wrapped in a robe." It was Samuel. In the
dialogue that ensues, Samuel rebukes Saul for
having disturbed him and brought him up from the
nether-world. To the question of what the future
will hold, Samuel answered that the Israelites will
be defeated by the Philistines and that, as he had
predicted while alive, David will become king in
Saul's place.

The striking features of this story are that Saul
had recourse to a practice that he himself had
prohibited, and the story assumes that this practice
worked. The story further shows that the dead
continue to exist as ghosts or spirits in the nether-
world and that they can be brought back to earth
by magical means. And finally it shows that these
ghosts or spirits have the ability to know the future,
something which in the sanctioned practices is
the function of the prophet. A less explicit but
similar picture emerges from other verses in the
Hebrew Bible. While the early books have little to
say about *she'ol*, more references appear in Isaiah,

Ezekiel, Psalms and Proverbs. But even they have little more to say than that the subterranean *she'ol* is the abode of the dead.

A second biblical eschatological theme is that of the Messiah.[4] While, at first, this belief seems to refer to the immediate restoration of the Davidic dynasty, the eternity of which had been promised, in the later books the expected restoration is postponed to the end of time. For example, Amos 9:11 reads: "In that day I will raise up the tabernacle of David that is fallen, and close up the breaches thereof, and I will raise up his ruins and I will build it as in the days of old." Or again, Jeremiah 23:5 states: "Behold the days come, saith the Lord, that I will raise unto David a righteous shoot, and he shall reign as king and prosper, and shall execute justice and righteousness in the land." In Isaiah 11:1-2, one hears, in still more idealistic fashion, of a time when peace will reign on earth and when" "there shall come forth a shoot out of the stock of Jesse [the father of David], and a twig shall grow forth out of his roots, and the spirit of the Lord shall rest upon him, the spirit of wisdom and understanding, the spirit of counsel and might, the spirit of knowledge and of the fear of the Lord."

Side by side with a belief in a personal Messiah, the bible speaks of messianic times, often introduced by the phrase "in that day" or "in those days." These times will be times of peace and tranquillity in which God will be king not only of Israel but of all the nations. "And there shall be one day, which shall be known as the Lord's," writes the prophet Zechariah (14:7-9), "[on which] the Lord shall be king over all the earth; in that day shall the Lord be one and His name one." In similar fashion the same prophet (14:16) writes: "and it shall come to pass that everyone that is left of all the nations that came against Jerusalem shall go up from year to year to worship the King, the Lord of hosts, and to keep the feast of Tabernacles."

Within the Hebrew canon the resurrection of the dead is mentioned explicitly for the first time in the book of Daniel (12:2-3). Speaking of a time of great trouble, such as had never been seen, Daniel predicted that then "many of them that sleep in the dust of the earth shall awake, some to everlasting life, some to reproaches and everlasting abhorrence." While within the canon, Daniel is the first book that mentions the resurrection of the dead explicitly, this notion is also discussed in such extra-canonical works as Enoch, and the Testament of the Twelve Patriarchs.

Chapter 12 of the book of Daniel is also important for an additional eschatological discussion, for it provides, in extremely enigmatic language, a date on which the Messiah will come. In later Jewish tradition, these dates became the occasion for calculating the date of arrival of messianic times. The very ambiguity of the language provided the opportunity to recalculate the date when the Messiah did not come at the envisaged time.

The Daniel passages (12:5-13) give three versions of the time when the Messiah will come, and later interpreters undertook to show that the three dates refer to the same time. Seeing in a vision an angelic being standing above the river and two other angelic beings standing at its banks, Daniel heard one of them asking the angelic being standing above the river: "How long will it be until the end of these awful things?" The angelic being standing above the river answered: "time, times, and a half" (*mo'ed, mo'adim, wa-ḥezi*. When Daniel did not understand the answer, he was given two other, no less enigmatic dates. According to one, the Messiah will come "a thousand two hundred and ninety days" after the cessation of the daily offering in the Temple, a time also when an appalling abomination is set up within it. According to the other passage, the Messiah will come in "one thousand three hundred and thirty five days." The rabbinic Sages disapproved of using these passages to calculate when the Messiah will come, so much so that they said: "Blast the bones of those who reckon out 'ends', for when their computed 'end' comes and he [the Messiah] does not come, they say he is not coming."[5] Yet the activity of computing the end never ceased.

How long it took for the doctrine of the resurrection of the dead to become normative in Jewish circles appears from the writings of Josephus (1st century B.C.E.) and from a story about the apostle Paul (d. 64 or 67 C.E.) appearing in the Acts of the Apostles. Writing in Greek for a Roman audience, Josephus undertook to describe the various Jewish sects largely in terms intelligible to his audience. Hence the beliefs of these groups had a central role in his exposition. Describing the life, practices, and beliefs of the three Jewish "philosophies"—Pharisees, Sadduccees, and Essenes—Josephus describes,

among other beliefs, their belief concerning the
resurrection of the dead.

With Platonic overtones, Josephus writes in
The Jewish Wars concerning the beliefs of the
Essenes that

> it is a fixed belief of theirs that the body
> is corruptible and its constituent matter
> impermanent, but that the soul is immortal
> and imperishable. Emanating from the finest
> ether, these souls become entangled, as it were,
> in the prison-house of the body, to which
> they are dragged down by a sort of natural
> spell; but when once they are released from the
> bonds of the flesh, then, as though liberated
> from a long servitude, they rejoice and are
> borne aloft.[6]

Comparing the beliefs of the Essenes with that
of the Greeks concerning the Isles of the Blessed
and Hades, Josephus continues that the Essenes
believe that the souls of the virtuous live in an
abode beyond the ocean, while the souls of the
wicked suffer a never ending punishment in a
murky and tempestuous dungeon. It is the purpose
of this exposition to establish the doctrine of the
immortality of the soul and to promote virtue and
keep people from vice. For

> the good are made better in their lifetime
> by the hope of reward after death, and the
> passions of the wicked are restrained by the

fear of ... never-ending punishment after their decease.[7]

Proceeding to the beliefs of the Pharisees, who are "considered the most accurate interpreters of the laws and who hold the position of the leading sect," Josephus writes that these believe that

> every soul is imperishable, but that of the good alone passes into another body, while the souls of the wicked suffer eternal punishment.[8]

The reference here does not seem to be to metempsychosis, but rather to the resurrection of the dead. By contrast the Sadducees believe that

> as for the persistence of the soul after death, penalties in the underworld, and rewards, they will have none of these.[9]

While Josephus does not spell out the reasons for the difference in the beliefs of the Sadduccees and the Pharisees, it is found in the fact that the former championed a literal reading of Scriptures, while the latter believed in its interpretation.

Returning once again to the "philosophies" of the three Jewish groups in his *Jewish Antiquities*, Josephus states that the Pharisees

> believe that the souls have power to survive death and that there are rewards and punishments

under the earth for those who have led lives of
virtue or vice; eternal imprisonment is the lot
of the evil souls, while the good souls receive
an easy passage to a new life.[10]

Concerning the beliefs of the Sadduccees, he writes
tersely that these "hold that the soul perishes along
with the body,"[11] and concerning the beliefs of
the Essenes he states that these believe that "the
soul is immortal."[12]

That the controversy concerning the resurrection
of the dead was still active at the time of Paul
appears from an episode reported in the book of
the Act of the Apostles. There it is reported that the
Jews had become restless at Paul's preaching, and
the Roman colonel had ordered that he should be
brought to the barracks for examination. When,
having been lashed, Paul claimed to be a Roman
citizen, the colonel decided to refer his case to
the high priest Ananias and the Jewish court (the
Sanhedrin). Having declared his innocence, Paul
continued his case. Here it is worthwhile to quote
the text:

Knowing that part of them [the court] were
Sadducees and part of them Pharisees, Paul
called out into the council 'Brothers, I am
a Pharisee and the son of Pharisees! It is for
my hope for the resurrection of the dead that
I am on trial!' When he said that, a dispute
arose between the Pharisees and the Sadducees
[who were members of the court] and the

> meeting was divided. For the Sadduccees hold
> that there is no resurrection and that there
> are no angels or spirits, while the Pharisees
> believe in all three.[13]

When then some of the Pharisees started to defend
Paul and the dispute became violent, the colonel had
Paul brought back to the Roman barracks.

With the decline of the Sadduccees and the activity of the rabbinic Sages, belief in the resurrection
of the dead became normative Jewish doctrine. But
that belief in resurrection had already taken hold
earlier appears from the apocryphal Second Book
of Maccabees, a book dealing with the deeds of
Judah Maccabee (second half of the first century
B.C.E.). After a battle with Gorgias, the governor of
Idumea, which Judah Maccabee had won, Judah's
army gathered the bodies of those who had fallen
in battle. When they discovered idolatrous amulets
under the shirts of those who had fallen, they
ascribed their death to the sin they had committed.
Judah then exhorted his people to remain free of
sin and he took up a collection for the Temple
in Jerusalem to provide a sin offering for those
who had fallen, thereby expressing his belief in the
resurrection of the dead. For, as the text reads,

> if he had not expected that those who had
> fallen would rise again, it would have been
> superfluous and foolish to pray for the dead; or
> if it was through regard for the splendid reward
> destined for those who fall asleep in godliness,

> it was a pious and holy thought. Therefore,
> he made atonement for the dead, so that they
> might be set free from their sin.[14]

While the resurrection of the dead and the advent of the Messiah constitute the major eschatological themes of Hebrew Scripture, several minor themes became part of the systematization of eschatology. One such is that the advent of the Messiah will be heralded by the prophet Elijah. This is based on the statement of the prophet Malachi (4:5) which reads: "Behold I will send you Elijah the prophet before the coming of the great and terrible day of the Lord."

One further eschatological theme emerges from Ezekiel's prophecy against Gog and Magog.[15] According to this prophecy, Gog, the ruler of the land of Magog, will assemble a great army, composed of many nations, and will march against the land of Israel. But the Lord in his anger will turn against Gog with pestilence, rain, fire, hail, and brimstone. Gog and his army will fall by the sword and he will be buried in the Land of Israel. All this will happen so that the people of Israel and all the nations shall know the glory of the Lord. These cataclysmic events shall be followed by the ingathering of the people of Israel so that they shall know that

> I am the Lord their God in that I caused them
> to go into captivity among the nations, and have

gathered them unto their own land and I will leave none of them any more there.[16]

By the time of the rabbinic Sages, known as Tannaim (1st and 2nd centuries of the Common Era), Jewish eschatological themes had become crystalized and formalized.[17] While we shall meet some of the rabbinic discussion when we come to the philosophers, some should be discussed in this context. One such is a Mishnah in Sanhedrin which reads:

> All Israelites have a part in the World to Come as it is said (Isaiah 60:21): 'Thy people also shall be all righteous, they shall inherit the land forever; the branch of My planting, the work of my hands, wherein I glory.'[18]

What is interesting about this Mishnah is that it mentions a term that does not appear in the biblical canon. It is the term The World to Come ('*olam ha-ba*'), and this is the term which now becomes central in later eschatological speculation. The meaning of this term is not made clear in this Mishnah and there is a good deal of rabbinic, and later philosophic, speculation about what exactly it means.

The same Mishnah continues:

> The following have no part in the World to Come: he who says there is no resurrection of

the dead, the Torah does not come from God,
and the Epicurean.

It is clear from this part of the Mishnah that
it attempts to fix certain principles of belief by
threatening that those who deny them will not have
a part in the World to Come. The very need to
set down these beliefs seems to be an indication
that there were those among the Jews who denied
them. It was, at least in part, this authoritative
Mishnah which helped to crystalize the belief in
resurrection. It should be added that part of this
Mishnah occurs in two forms. In one form it reads
that one must believe in resurrection, but in another
form it reads that one must believe not only in
resurrection, but also that resurrection is already
mentioned in the Torah.

Another much discussed saying is that of Rav,
a third century Babylonian teacher. Invoking the
image of a banquet he writes:

> (The World to Come is unlike this World). In the
> World to Come there is no eating or drinking,
> no propagation of the species, no business, no
> jealousy or hatred, and no competition, but the
> righteous sit, their crowns on their heads and
> enjoy the radiance of the divine presence as it is
> said (Exodus 24:11) 'and they beheld God and
> did eat and drink.'[19]

While later interpreters, as we shall see, differ
in their interpretation of the text, this Mishnah

appears to foster a more spiritual conception of the afterlife.

One of the themes that engaged the thought world of the rabbinic Sages was the conditions under which the Messiah will come. Again it should be noted that, while the eschatological terminology was reasonably fixed, it received a variety of interpretations. More than that, at times it was used for moral or religious instruction or to make an exhortatory point. We read, for example, that the Messiah will come only in a generation that is wholly worthy or in one that is wholly guilty.[20] Or, again, Rabbi Simeon bar Yoḥai is quoted as saying that the Messiah will come if Israel will keep two Sabbaths according to the Law.[21] Repentance as a condition for the advent of the Messiah was also advocated by a number of rabbinic Sages. One such statement reads that "great is repentance for it brings deliverance nearer, as it is said (Isaiah 59:20), 'there comes to Zion a deliverer, and to those who turn from transgression in Jacob.'"[22]

Whether repentance was a necessary condition for the advent of the Messiah also became an occasion for rabbinic controversy. Thus we hear of a discussion between R. Eliezer ben Hyrcanus and R. Joshua ben Ḥananiah. The former maintained that should Israel not repent they would never be delivered, while the latter maintained that whether or not the Israelites repented they would be delivered at a 'fixed time'.[23] According to the latter view, God had set a time for the advent of the Messiah within cosmic chronology—two thousand years emptiness, two thousand years Torah, and

two thousand years messianic age.[24] The notion
that the Messiah will come at a fixed time gave
rise to speculations concerning the time of his
arrival. When the Messiah did not arrive at the
calculated time, people revised their calculations.
That those calculations were condemned we have
already seen earlier, but this did not prevent such
calculations.

Some rabbinic Sages concentrated on moral and
religious decline as a sign that the coming of the
Messiah was at hand. For example Rabbi Judah
ben Ilai said: "In the generation in which the Son
of David comes, the meeting house will become a
brothel, Galilee will be devastated and the Gaulan
laid waste, the inhabitants of the border will go
around from city to city and find no compassion,
the learning of scholars will be stench in man's
nostrils, the countenance of the generation will
be as impudent as a dog's, and truth cannot be
found."[25] Rabbi Neḥemiah, a disciple of Rabbi
Akiba is quoted as saying, "Before the Days of the
Messiah poverty will increase and high prices will
prevail; the vine will give its fruit, but the wine will
spoil. The whole empire will turn to heresy, and
there will be no reprehension of it."[26]

The theme that the coming of the Messiah will be
preceded by the prophet Elijah, mentioned sketchily
by the prophet Malachi, received elaboration in
the rabbinic literature. In addition to assigning to
Elijah such legal functions as settling controversies
concerning what was clean and unclean, and
determining who of the Israelites was of pure stock,
later authorities make it his mission to bring Israel

to repentance. The Pirkei de-Rabbi Eliezer quotes Rabbi Judah as saying, "Israel will not make the great repentance until Elijah comes."[27]

That the coming of the Messiah will be preceded by a period of great calamity was so much part of eschatological thinking that it gave rise to a special term—the travail of the Messiah (*ḥeblei mashiaḥ*).[28] It is one of the three punishments—the other two being the days of Gog and Magog and the judgment day—from which those who observe the Sabbath properly are saved.[29] Basing themselves on the verse in Amos (9:10) "All the sinners of my people will die by the sword that say, the evil will not overtake nor confront us," which precedes the prophet's messianic expectations, some rabbinic Sages argue that the punishment of sinners will take place during the time of the "travail of the Messiah." For example, Rabbi Ḥiyya bar Abba states that "shortly before the days of the Messiah there will come a great pestilence, and the wicked will meet their end in it."[30] Or again, comparing the messianic deliverance to the Exodus from Egypt, it is held that just as, according to tradition, the wicked of Israel died in the darkness of the third day, so will the wicked of Israel die in the cataclysmic period that precedes the days of the Messiah.[31]

While, as we have seen, Rav had a rather spiritual conception of the eschatological banquet, others had a more physical one. Basing themselves on the description of Behemoth and Leviathan, terrestrial and maritime monsters respectively, in Job 40-41, some of the Sages held that these would serve as food for the eschatological banquet. Thus we read that God created a pair of Leviathans, but when he envisages how much harm they may do, he castrated the male and killed and pickled the female to preserve her flesh for the eschatological banquet.[32] Since the banquet required wine, God created the wine of the messianic banquet in the six days of creation.[33]

The fruitfulness of the land of Israel was another eschatological theme. In an opinion, the literal interpretation of which was criticized later by Maimonides, it is stated that every grain of wheat will be as large as the kidneys of a large bullock, and that each grape will yield as much wine as a person would want.[34] According to another Sage, grapes will be so large that each grape will yield thirty jars of wine. According to still another opinion, the land will bring forth rolls of bread and garments of fine wool.[35]

A further feature of messianic times was the return of the Israelites to their own land from their dispersion and exile. Mentioned in the prophecy of Jeremiah, this notion receives further elaboration from the rabbinic Sages. The Jeremiah passage (30:3) reads: "For, lo, days are coming, saith the Lord, when I will turn the captivity of my People Israel and Judah … and I will return them to the land which I gave to their forefathers and they shall possess it." Comparing the return of the people of Israel to the Exodus from Egypt, Jeremiah (23: 7-8) had predicted that people shall no longer say, "'as the Lord liveth who brought the children of Israel out of the land of Egypt,' but, 'as the Lord liveth, who led up and brought the posterity of the Children of Israel from the northern lands and from all the lands whither I drove them away'; and they shall dwell on their own soil."[36]

One more theme that makes its appearance is that of a second Messiah, the Messiah son of Joseph. While he is not mentioned explicitly in the biblical text, allusions to him are found in two biblical passages. Commenting on the verse in Zechariah (12:10) which reads: "And they shall mourn for him [that has been slain], as one mourneth for his only son, and shall be in bitterness for him as one that is in bitterness for his first-born," one rabbinic Sage interprets that the mourning is for the Messiah son of Joseph who had been killed.[37] An allusion to the Messiah son of Joseph is also found in the verse from Obadiah (v. 18) which reads: "and the house of Jacob shall be a fire, and the house of Joseph a flame, and the house of Esau for stubble, and thy shall kindle in them and devour them; and there shall not be any remaining of the house of Esau." Since in the language of the rabbinic Sages Esau becomes a symbol for with Rome, Rabbi Samuel ben Naḥman suggests, rather vaguely, that Esau (Rome) will be delivered only into the hand of the descendent of Joseph. While the theory is not fully developed, it appears that the career and death of Messiah son of Joseph will precede the coming of Messiah son of David.[38]

Side by side with the belief in the coming of the Messiah, which had political overtones, there existed a more universalistic conception of the messianic age. Already expressed in some of the prophetic writings, it is now no longer a human being who is

king, but it is God himself. Speaking of the Lord's
day, when there will be no day or night, the Prophet
Zechariah (14:9) states that "on that day the Lord
shall be King over all the earth; on that day the Lord
shall be one and His name one."

Saadiah Gaon

Saadiah Gaon (882-942) was by general agreement
the first medieval Jewish philosopher. Born in
Fayume, Egypt, he reached the high point of his
career as head of the Yeshivah (rabbinical seminary)
in Surah, near Baghdad.[39] A prolific author, Saadiah
composed works on grammar, translated the bible
into Arabic and commented on it, wrote on prayer,
was the author of legal responsa, and wrote on
the calendar. A polemicist by nature, he entered
a controversy concerning the calendar which he
decided in favor of the Babylonian community
against that of Palestine, wrote against a biblical
critic Ḥiwi ha-Balkhi, and presented the Rabbinite
case against the Karaites, a Jewish sect that accepted
the bible but rejected the interpretation of the
Rabbis. But most important for our purpose, he
was the author of a philosophic-theological work,
entitled *Book of Opinions and Beliefs*, in which he
presented his philosophy-theology.

Saadiah's time was marked by intellectual turbu-
lence not only among Muslims, but also among
Christians and Jews in the Islamic world. The
religious and intellectual situation is well described
by a Spanish cleric who visited Baghdad.[40] On
his return trip he visited a colleague in Kairwan

who wanted to hear about the intellectual life in Baghdad, particularly about the assemblies of the *Kalâm*. While, as we shall see, *Kalâm* describes a philosophic-theological movement to which Saadiah belonged, the term also describes public assemblies devoted to the discussion of philosophic and theological topics. Describing to his Kairwan colleague two such assemblies that he had attended, the Spanish theologian reports that there were present not only representatives of various Islamic sects, but also "unbelievers, Magians (dualists), materialists, atheists, Jews, and Christians, in short, unbelievers of all kinds." Once the hall had become filled, reports the Spaniard, one of the unbelievers arose and instructed the assembly "the conditions [of our meeting] are known to all. You Muslims, are not allowed to argue from your books and prophetic traditions since we deny both. Everybody, therefore, has to limit himself to rational arguments. The whole assembly applauded these words." His host took the Spaniard to another assembly of the *Kalâm*, but "I found the same calamity there," the Spaniard concluded his report.

The report of the Muslim is confirmed for the Jewish community in Saadiah's own work. Saadiah, describing the reasons for doubts and unbelief of his contemporaries, writes:

> For I saw in this age of mine many believers whose beliefs were not pure and whose convictions were not sound, while many deniers of the faith boasted of their corruption and looked

down upon the devotees of the truth although
they were themselves in error.[41]

To combat these, Saadiah wrote his *Book of
Opinions and Beliefs*. In a picturesque metaphor,
he compared his contemporaries to men who were
sunk in seas of doubt and overwhelmed by waves of
confusion, and there was no swimmer who could
rescue them and bring them to shore. He writes:

> But inasmuch as my Lord had granted me some
> knowledge by which I might come to their
> assistance and had endowed me with some
> ability that I could put at their disposal for
> their benefit, I thought it was my duty to help
> them therewith and my obligation to direct
> them to the truth.[42]

Saadiah considered himself that swimmer who
would safely bring them to shore. While Saadiah's
book contains many philosophic arguments, it
is addressed to a wider audience. He proposes
to formulate his views in simple terms, use easy
language, and make use of only general proofs
and arguments. "The contents [of the book] will
be plain to follow," he concludes, "…and he who
diligently studies the book may thereby arrive
at equity and truth."[43] Further evidence for the
intellectual complexity of the period is provided
by the fact that whenever Saadiah discusses an
issue he provides not only an exposition of his
own opinion but also a critique of divergent views.

For the case of creation he provides no fewer than twelve cosmogonic theories (three are really epistemological theories) with which he disagrees.[44] While it was held at one time that some of these are hypothetical, more recent research has shown that they were actually held by Saadiah's contemporaries or predecessors.

In his philosophic orientation Saadiah belonged to a movement known as Mu'tazilite Kalâm. A good deal has been written about the origin and meaning of this term, but for our purposes it is best to describe the adherents of this movements as dialectical theologians.[45] Having followers among Muslims and Jews, the Mu'tazilites undertook to solve scriptural problems by philosophic means. Since they took philosophic arguments wherever they found them, their speculations had an eclectic rather than systematic character. On the philosophic side an interest in two problems marked Mu'tazilite thought. One such is the problem of divine unity. If God is one, how can he be described by many attributes? The books of the Mu'tazilites begin with proofs of the creation of the world, which lead to proofs of the existence of the creator. Saadiah in his various writings provides nine such proofs. From proofs for creation Mu'tazilites proceed to the problem of divine attributes. Here the issue was to reconcile the scriptural notion that God is absolutely one with his description by means of many attributes. Through interpreting divine attributes in accordance with ordinary linguistic usage, Mu'tazilites undertook to show that such attributes can be predicated of God without introducing multiplicity into his essence.

A second philosophic theme was that of divine justice and the related problem of human freedom. Here the issue was that divine omnipotence seems to imply that God was the direct cause of everything that happens in the world, including human actions. But if this were the case, how can God justly punish people for their misdeeds or reward them for the good deeds they do? To obviate this difficulty, Muʿtazilites interpreted divine omnipotence to mean that God has the ability to be the direct cause of everything that happens in the world, but they presented evidence that for the case of human actions, God delegated his power to human beings, that is, human beings are the direct causes of their actions. To support this claim, Muʿtazilites presented two arguments. One such was that human beings felt themselves free to determine their own actions, and this sense was stronger than any arguments for determinism. The second argument was one from divine justice. That God, for example, should punish sinners who had no control over their own actions went against the basic principle that God was just and that God's justice had to be similar to human justice. The problem of divine power was solved by distinguishing between God's ability to delegate his causal power and his exercising it directly. From their concern with these two problems, the Muʿtazilites were known as "The Proponents of Divine Unity and Divine Justice."

Since the speculative issues discussed so far are philosophic in nature, Saadiah found no difficulty in incorporating them in his *Book of Opinions and Beliefs*. In typical Mu'tazilite fashion he begins his work with four proofs for the creation of the world leading to the existence of God, then proceeds to the question of divine attributes, and concludes this section by discussing divine law, God's communication with mankind.[46] In the next section of his work Saadiah proceeds to the second kalâmic problem, divine justice. Beginning with empirical arguments for the existence of free will—those from sense perception—Saadiah presents a variety of arguments based on the incompatibility of the deterministic interpretation of divine omnipotence (and omniscience) with God's justice.[47]

While Saadiah's relation to Mu'tazilite discussion of divine unity and justice is clear, his relation to the remaining three principles of the Mu'tazilites appear to be more problematic. While George Vajda sees Mu'tazilite influences even here,[48] it seems that Saadiah turns here to more specifically Jewish concepts. The third Mu'tazilite principle is that of "the promise and the threat" according to which a Muslim guilty of a serious offense who dies without repentance will suffer the torments of hell for eternity—this according to the threats uttered against him in the Koran. The fourth principle is that of the "intermediary state" according to which a sinful Muslim cannot be classified here on earth as a believer or unbeliever but belongs to the separate category that of "sinner" (*fâsiq*). Finally, according to the fifth principle, a Muslim is "to command the good and forbid the evil," that is to uphold the Islamic Law and oppose impiety. In short, he is to

take part actively in public affairs. While one can
see some similarity between the list of personality
types in the fifth treatise of the *Book of Opinions and
Beliefs* and the various kinds of sinners described in
the Islamic version of Mu'tazilite Kalâm, it seems
to be fair to say that these similarities are rather
superficial.

One more methodological point needs to be
discussed. As we have seen it was a principle of
Mu'tazilite Kalâm that every opinion had to be
supported by rational argument, but it was equally
a principle that every opinion was to be supported
by a scriptural verse and by a statement taken
from religious tradition. For the case of Islam,
this meant support had to be gathered from the
Koran and Hadith; for the case of Judaism, it
meant that support had to come from verses of the
Hebrew Bible and from the teachings of the rabbinic
Sages. By this method was shown the confluence of
religious tradition and rational argument.

With these preliminary observations we can now
turn to Saadiah's eschatological teachings. Here it
should be noted, first of all, that a large portion
of the *Book of Opinions and Beliefs* is devoted to
matters of eschatology. If we exclude the tenth
treatise of the work, which is devoted to practical
instruction, and if we add the chapter on the nature
of the human soul, which is preliminary to teachings
about eschatology, a full four of the nine chapters of
the work are devoted to matters of eschatology. This
would seem to show how important eschatological
teachings had become by the time of Saadiah and

how necessary it was to present such teachings in a clear and authoritative manner.

As background for his discussion of specific eschatological themes, Saadiah begins by describing the nature of the human soul. Once again the variety of opinions that he lists is striking. Noting that there are eleven theories concerning the nature of the soul, Saadiah mentions that he has disposed of four of these in the chapter of his work devoted to creation.[49] Of these, two are especially noteworthy. One of these is a discussion of the nature of the soul based on the theory of emanation according to which God brought the world into being out of his own substance.[50] Among the several arguments presented against such emanation is the following. It is unreasonable that God who possesses neither form nor attributes of quality, time, or place can be changed through emanation in such a way that, as emanated substance, he now possesses corporeal attributes. To put it in another way, emanation cannot explain how emanated creatures acquire attributes of corporeality. Another argument is directed against the opinion of the dualists according to which just as the world came to be from two eternal principles—one the principle of good, the other the principle of evil—so the human soul came to be from the same two principles.[51] The underlying principle of the dualists is that divergent acts cannot come from the same cause. To counter this argument Saadiah presents instances in which clearly divergent acts can come from one principle. One such is that a person may be enraged and angry at one time, and satisfied and forgiving at

another. Yet it is the same person that exhibits these
contrary states.

Having disposed of six other theories concerning
the soul according to which the soul is an accident,
consists of air, fire, a rational part located in the
heart and a vital part spread throughout the body,
two kinds of air, and blood, Saadiah proceeds to
his own theory.[52] According to it, the soul, like
everything in the world, is created, and it is created
when the human body comes to be. It is physical,
but its substance is purer than that of the celestial
spheres. It receives luminosity through a light
received from God and it is through this luminosity
that it possesses intellect. Saadiah's description
of the soul is derived from two arguments: one
rational, the other Scriptural. According to a rational
argument, it is the case that when the soul leaves
the body, the body no longer possesses wisdom or
forethought. Hence these cannot be properties of
the body. Similarly, were the substance of the soul
the same as that of the celestial bodies, it would
no more possesses reason than they do. Hence the
substance of the soul must be finer, clearer, purer
and simpler than that of the celestial body. The
luminosity of the soul is argued from such verses as
"The wise shine as the brightness of the firmament"
(Daniel 12:3). Just as the stars illumine the celestial
spheres, so the soul of the righteous have a brilliance
of their own.

While the body is required as an instrument
for intellectual cognition, thinking belongs to the
essence of the soul. Evidence is provided by the
case of the blind man who in his dream can see,

though he does not have any sense perception. In fact, sense perception is provided by the soul to the body. Invoking a distinction that has its roots in Plato, Saadiah distinguishes among three faculties of the soul: reason, appetite and courage. These are not, as some held, separate souls but rather faculties of the one soul. Finally, the seat of this soul is the heart, not, as some thought, that some of these faculties have their seat in the heart, others have their seat in other parts of the body. The soul has its seat in the heart since nerves controlling sensation and motion issue from the heart. To be sure, many nerves issue from the brain, but these have only a bodily function and do not participate in the activities of the soul.

Having presented his definition of the soul, Saadiah turns to objections by certain unnamed opponents.[53] These argue that God was unjust in placing the soul that in its purity exceeds the heavenly bodies into the gross human body. To answer these opponents Saadiah states that acts of injustice cannot be predicated of the Creator. There are three possibilities for acts of injustice and none of these applies to him. One of these is a person's fear of the object of his injustice, another is greed for something that the object may possess, and the third is ignorance concerning the truth about the object of injustice. Since, however, God cannot said to be afraid, desirous, or ignorant, none of these causes of injustice can be applied to him. Saadiah goes on to support these statements by a number of Scriptural verses.

The soul and body constitute one agent and it is for this reason that they are rewarded and punished together.[54] To be sure, there are those who hold that reward and punishment are given to the soul alone, others maintain that they are only given to the body, and still others state that they are given to the human bones. But all of these, Saadiah maintains, come to their opinions through the misinterpretation of biblical verses. Typical of the first group are those who place their description of the soul on such verses as "The soul that sinneth, it shall die" (Ezekiel 18:4), but they ignore such verses as "But the soul that eateth of the flesh" (Leviticus 7:20) in which the term "soul" can only refer to the body. Such interpretations, Saadiah explains, show the interpreter's ignorance of how biblical language functions. For when an action is performed by several agents, the bible may describe it by means of the first agent alone

Speaking of the life span of a human being, Saadiah turns to a more naturalistic interpretation.[55] The ordinary life span of a person is determined by the constitution of his body, the average life span being seventy years. God, however, may extend or diminish it thirty years in either direction. The life span of the pious may be extended, while the life span of the sinner may be diminished. Natural catastrophes, such as a plague, may also diminish a person's life span. To account for the shortening of the life of the pious or the increase of the life of the sinner, Saadiah invokes the principle of "afflictions of love" (*yissurin shel ahabah*), a principle which he had discussed earlier in chapter five. According to this principle, the shortened life span of the pious may be rewarded in the World to Come ('*olam ha-ba*) while the extended life span of the wicked may be compensation for some good he did in this world.

To describe the death of a human being, Saadiah turns to a description in the Talmud which, in turn, is supported with biblical passages.[56] At the moment of death an angel sent by God appears to the dying person. The body of the angel is composed of yellow fire, while his eyes are made of blue fire. In the angel's hand is a drawn sword aimed at the dying person. At the sight of the angel the dying person is terrified and the soul leaves the body.

Having described the separation of body and soul by death, Saadiah raises a number of questions concerning the soul.[57] If the soul, as has been argued, is physical, why can its departure not be perceived by the senses? Turning to his earlier discussion, he answers that since the substance of the soul is more subtle than the celestial spheres, just as these cannot be perceived, so can the soul not be perceived. Offering an analogy, Saadiah states that if a burning candle is inside ten glass vessels, only the candle but not the vessels can be seen, so the soul because of its subtlety cannot be seen.

Turning to matters more immediately eschatological, Saadiah inquires into the state of the soul after death.[58] Citing a verse from Proverbs he maintains that the disembodied soul is stored up until the time of retribution. Speaking somewhat vaguely, he states that the souls of the righteous will go up, while the souls of the wicked will descend below. Besides citing biblical verse, he also cites the well-known rabbinic saying: "The souls of the righteous are stored beneath the Throne of Glory, while the souls of the wicked wander about in the world" (Shabbat 152b). The soul, however, does not immediately reach this state. During the period immediately after its departure from the body, the soul remains without a fixed abode, and during this period it experiences much pain in accordance with its deeds here on earth. This period lasts until the body is decayed. It is then that the soul moves to its abode either above or below. As it is written, "But his flesh grieveth for him and his soul mourneth over him" (Job 14:22). In rabbinic language the immediate state after death is known as *Din ha-Keber* (The Judgement of the Grave) or *Ḥibbut ha-Keber* (The Beating of the Grave).

The separated souls will exist in their assigned place until God has created all the souls which in his wisdom he has decided to create.[59] At that time, known as the end of the existence of the world, God will reunite the souls and their bodies and then will judge them. Saadiah will discuss this state later on.

Returning once again to theories of the soul with which he disagrees, Saadiah holds that according to one group the soul ceases to exist, while according to another group the soul returns to the source from which it came.[60] Referring to his earlier refutation of these views, Saadiah considers metempsychosis, according to which the soul of a human being passes into the body of another human being or, according to some, even into the body of an animal.

Enumerating four reasons that bring the proponents of metempsychosis to their opinion, Saadiah lists as the most interesting of these the sufferings of small children. Maintaining that God is just and could not let small children suffer for no reason, believers in metempsychosis argue that these sufferings occur for misdeeds done in their former life. To rebut this argument Saadiah refers to an earlier discussion in his work. According to the view expressed there, the affliction of apparently righteous or innocent people is to increase their reward in the afterlife. In the rabbinic tradition, on which Saadiah relies, such afflictions are known as "afflictions of love" (*yissurin shel ahabah*). Misunderstanding of biblical passages is another basis for the opinion of those who believe in metempsychosis.

Having discussed the nature of the soul, Saadiah proceeds to the resurrection of the dead. Here it must be noted that we have two divergent versions of the Arabic text, one contained in a Leningrad manuscript, the other in an Oxford manuscript. The Hebrew translation of Judah Ibn Tibbon is based on the Leningrad manuscript.[61] As is to be expected, Saadia's theory of resurrection is primarily based on traditional sources, though rational arguments are not lacking.

Saadiah begins by stating that all Jews agree that the resurrection of the dead will occur at the time of messianic redemption.[62] There are some who place the resurrection at the time of the transition from this world to the next, but this is a minority. The possibility of resurrection is argued from the creation of the world, for which Saadiah has offered a number of philosophic arguments.[63] Just as God created the world out of nothing, so can he reunite soul and body.

Apparently taking issue with those who deny the physical resurrection of the dead and who hold that this doctrine must be interpreted metaphorically, Saadiah argues for its literal acceptance.[64] There are only four instances in which a biblical or rabbinic doctrine must be interpreted in non-literal fashion, and none of these applies to the case of the resurrection of the dead. One of these is if the statement is contradicted by sense perception. Citing the biblical verse "And the man called his wife's name Eve, because she was the mother of all living" (Genesis 3:20), Saadiah interprets that the term "living" can only refer to human beings. Hence, "living" must have the restricted meaning "human beings." A second instance in which a biblical verse must be interpreted in non-literal fashion occurs when the literal meaning is contrary to reason. Here Saadiah's example is "For the Lord thy God is a devouring fire, a jealous God" (Deuteronomy 4:24). This verse must be interpreted to mean that God's punishment is like a devouring fire, for fire is something created, defective, and subject to extinction. None of these attributes can be predicated of God. A third instance in which a biblical verse must be interpreted is when it is contradicted by another biblical verse. The verse "Ye shall not try the Lord your God, as ye tried Him in Massah" (Deuteronomy 6:16) is contradicted by the verse "And try me now herewith … if I will not open you the windows of heaven" (Malachi

3:10). The two verses, Saadiah interprets, refer to two different cases. Invoking a third verse, he holds that both verses prohibit testing God's ability to do a certain thing, as was done at Massah. The second verse, however, gives us permission to ask God whether he can create a certain miracle. The fourth case is one in which there is an oral tradition which attaches a non-literal meaning to the biblical text. Here the case is that a punishment can consist of forty stripes. However, the biblical statement reading "Forty stripes he may give him" (Deuteronomy 25:3) is to be interpreted, according to oral tradition, to mean that the punishment must be limited to thirty-nine stripes. Saadiah concludes that since none of the four cases applies to the resurrection of the dead, this doctrine must be accepted literally.

Having shown that the doctrine of the resurrection of the dead must be accepted in literal fashion, Saadiah supports it by a number of biblical references.[65] Here he sets out to show that while the main text supporting resurrection is found in the book of Daniel, the principle is found much earlier. Allusion to the resurrection is already found in the book of Deuteronomy. Moses' poem which predicts the fortunes of the children of Israel contains the verse "I kill and I make alive; I have wounded and I heal" (Deuteronomy 32:39). Because of the chronological structure of the poem, "I kill and I make alive" must refer to the resurrection of the dead, for just as the body which is healed after it has been wounded is the same body, so the body that dies is the body that is resurrected. Turning to other

biblical evidence, Saadiah accepts the parable of the
dry bones found in the book of Ezekiel (chapter
37) as teaching the resurrection of the dead,[66] just
as he accepts the prophet Isaiah's promises "Thy
dead shall live, my dead bodies shall arise" (26:19)
as referring to resurrection.

The most explicit support comes, however, from
the book of Daniel 12:2, which reads: "And many of
them that sleep in the dust of the earth shall awake,
some to everlasting life and some to reproaches."[67]
In stating "and many of them" the verse teaches that
only Israelites will be resurrected, not all mankind.
"Some to everlasting life and some to reproaches"
does not teach that some of those resurrected will
be punished, but rather that only those that will be
rewarded will be resurrected.

The resurrection of the dead is supported not
only by biblical verses but by rabbinic sayings as
well.[68] For example, concerning one who denies
the resurrection of the dead, it is stated in the
Talmud that "since he does not believe in the
resurrection of the dead, therefore he shall not have
any portion in it."

Having argued for the resurrection of the dead
through reason, Scripture, and rabbinic sayings,
Saadiah goes on to consider the nature of resurrection and certain puzzle cases concerning it. One
such is that if one considers several generations of
human beings and assumes that they die, it would
seem to be the case that their disintegrated bodies
or parts of them would have to be used to constitute
the bodies of the next generations. Since then part
of the bodies existing at any one time would have

been re-used, how can they be used at the time of the resurrection?

To answer the question, Saadiah uses a parable.[69] Let it be assumed that a person owns a vessel worth a thousand drachma and that there are no other vessels. If the vessel is broken and the person wishes to make another vessel, he must use parts of the vessels he originally possessed. Should it, however, be the case that he possesses unlimited amounts of silver, he could make a vessel from the store of silver he possesses and he could reconstitute the broken vessel from its own parts. Turning to a more scientific account, Saadiah states that according to his calculation, the quantity of elements are more than sufficient to reconstitute any human body without having to use the same element twice.

An apparently more difficult case is presented by a human being eaten by a lion, the lion then drowns, is eaten by a fish, the fish is caught and eaten by a second man, who in the end is burned and turned into ashes. The fire in the last case, it would seem, destroys the elements of the first man completely so that there is no material element from which the first person can be resurrected. The example, argues Saadiah, is mistaken, for there is no element that can be destroyed completely.[70] Since God has promised the resurrection of human beings, it follows that in spite of all the changes, the parts of the original human body remain so that from them the body may be reconstituted.

Turning to other puzzling questions, Saadiah asks whether those who are resurrected will recognize and be recognized by members of their families.[71] Citing

a rabbinic passage and biblical verses, he answers in
the affirmative. Will those who die afflicted with a
blemish be resurrected with the blemish or will they
be resurrected cured? Saadiah answers by citing the
rabbinic passage "They will rise from their graves
with their blemish attached to them and then be
cured" (Sanhedrin 91b).[72]

In a more philosophic vein Saadiah asks whether
those who are resurrected at the time of redemption
have the ability to sin.[73] Should they not have the
power to sin, they would lack free choice; should
they have the power to sin and indeed should they
have sinned, they would die and be punished.
Drawing a parallel to angels and prophets, he comes
to the conclusion that since God promised reward
in the World to Come to those who are resurrected,
it follows that they cannot sin. Will those who are
resurrected receive reward for the service they render
God after they are resurrected? Saadiah answers
in the affirmative. Just as those who worship God
in the World to Come will be rewarded for their
service, so those who worship God after they are
resurrected will receive their reward.

Finally Saadiah turns to the question whether
those in whose lifetime resurrection takes place will
die or not. There are three opinions to the third of
which Saadiah inclines.[74] According to one of these,
those living at the time of redemption will not die
but will be transported to the World to Come at the
appropriate time. According to another opinion,
those living at the time of the redemption will
live only a short time, then will die and will be
immediately resurrected so that they may be on

par with those who are resurrected. Finally, there are those who hold that those living at the time of the resurrection will live a long life, but will not live until the time of the World to Come. As his reason Saadiah states that the purpose of the resurrection is that those resurrected will witness the redemption, which purpose is fulfilled by those who are living at that time.

For his description of the time of the redemption, Saadiah turns primarily to biblical and rabbinic sources.[75] Here his main concern is to argue that while this doctrine is expressed primarily by later sources, references in earlier sources—he has in mind the Pentateuch—are not lacking. To prove the point he cites the statement "The Lord thy God will turn thy captivity" (Deuteronomy 30:3). One of the more philosophic arguments that Saadiah offers is that of God's justice. To be sure, some of the suffering of the Jews is punishment, part of it is trial, but whatever the case may be, the time of suffering must be limited, and the end of that time is the time of redemption.

Jewish tradition speaks of two time limits for the arrival of the time of redemption. According to one of these, the redemption will occur when the Jewish people will repent; according to the other it will occur at a fixed time, known as the end. Whichever of the two occurs first will mark the time of redemption.[76] The notion that redemption will occur at a fixed time gave rise to regular calculations throughout history, most of these designed to show that the time of redemption was at hand. To prevent despair, the rabbinic sages disapproved of such calculations, but such calculations continued throughout Jewish history. Saadiah was no exception.

To calculate the time of the redemption, scholars turned to some enigmatic passages in the book of Daniel. As we have already seen, Daniel in a vision saw three angels standing at the river, one above it, the other two standing at its banks. Asked by one of those standing at the river's banks when the redemption will come, the angel standing above the river answered "time, times, and a half." Daniel was puzzled by the answer, but the angel standing above the river explained to him that his language was enigmatic so that the common people would not be worried about the coming of the end. To put Daniel's mind at ease the angel explained further that the appointed time would come in 1335 days. While the angel speaks of days, he means to indicate years. In still another passage it is predicted that the end will occur 1290 days after the burnt offering in the Temple has ceased. This event occurred 45 years after Daniel's vision. Again, the total is 1335 years. All three dates, Saadiah interprets, are the same, and he undertakes to demonstrate this as well as determine what the intended date would be.[77]

Saadiah begins the calculation by stating that in the phrase "time, times, and a half," the term "time" refers to the period during which the people of Israel was independent. This period amounts to 890 years: 480 years before the building of the First Temple ("time") and 410 years as the time the Temple lasted ("times"). Half of the total figure is 445 years, so that the length of "time, times, and a half" amounts to 1335 years. This figure is the same as that explicitly stated as the last part of the prophecy. On the basis of these calculations what will be the year of the messianic redemption? Putting together the chronology with which he was familiar, Saadiah comes to the conclusion that the year of the redemption will be 4,725 of the Jewish calendar, which corresponds to the year 965 of the common era. Saadiah reaches this conclusion in the following manner. From the creation of the world until the exodus from Egypt there elapsed 2,448 years; from the exodus from Egypt until the building of the First Temple there were 400 years; the First Temple lasted 410 years; from the destruction of the First Temple to the first year of Darius, the year in which Daniel saw his vision, there were 52 years. This brings the total to 3,390 years. If to this we add the 1,335 years of Daniel's vision, we arrive at the year 4,725 according to the Hebrew calendar, 23 years after Saadiah's death.

While Saadiah can accept that the redemption will come when the Children of Israel have repented, he finds it more difficult to accept that the redemption will come at a fixed time, regardless of whether or not the Jews repented.[78] To obviate this difficulty, he turns to some of the subsidiary aspects of Jewish eschatological thought. If repentance is not done voluntarily, it will be forced by God, that is, God will produce misfortune and disasters as a result of which the Israelites will repent. There will appear in Upper Galilee the Messiah son of Joseph. He will gather around himself members of the Jewish nation with whom he will go to Jerusalem. After some time has passed, a warrior named Armilus will conquer the city, killing many of its inhabitants. Among the slain will be the Messiah son of Joseph. Great misfortunes will befall the Jews, greatest among them the dissolution of their relation to the gentile nations. As a result of these misfortunes, Jews will repent, but many will leave their faith. To those who will remain faithful, Elijah the prophet will appear and redemption will follow.

Regardless of which eschatological scheme will come to be, the Messiah son of David will appear suddenly.[79] Should the Jews have repented and the Messiah son of Joseph should not appear, the Messiah son of David will march with an army against Jerusalem, take the city, and kill Armilus, in whose hands Jerusalem will be at that time. Developing a further eschatological theme, Saadiah describes the war of Gog and Magog. Hearing of the good fortune of the Jews under the rule of Messiah son of David, Gog and Magog plan to attack his kingdom. Aware of these plans, the Messiah son of David gathers an army from many nations with which to attack and defeat the forces of Gog and Magog.

Those from the nations who join the war against Gog and Magog, Saadiah continues, are of two kinds: those who are sinners and those who enter the faith.[80] Four kinds of punishments will befall the sinners and four kinds of reward those who enter the faith. Some sinners will be punished by fire, sulphur, and brimstones raining down on them, others will perish by each others' swords, still others' flesh will rot and their bones will disintegrate, and, finally, those who are left will lose part of their bodies so that they may go out and report to the world the great punishment that has befallen them. Just as there are four kinds of punishment for the sinners, so are their four kinds of rewards for those who join the faith. Those who are most distinguished will become servants in the homes of the children of Israel, those less distinguished will become servants in cities and villages, still others will work in vineyards and fields, and those who are left will return to their countries but will be subjugated to the Jews. Those of the nations will, as Scripture requires, come to the Temple in Jerusalem to celebrate the feast of Tabernacles, but rain will be withheld from those who refuse to come.

Once the Messiah son of David has arrived, the resurrection of the dead will take place.[81] If the Messiah son of Joseph will have been slain, having been a righteous man, he will be among the first to be resurrected. Then the temple of Jerusalem will be restored, but this one unlike the first two Temples, in accordance with its description in the book of Ezekiel. The entire land of Israel will be inhabited, so that no desert will be left. The light of God's presence will shine and prophecy will come to all the Jews. Those who have been redeemed will willingly serve God and rebel against him no more. Pestilence and disease will disappear and so will sadness and sorrow. Messianic times will be times of gladness and joy, obedience and service to God.

One of the troublesome theses against the normative description of messianic times was the opinion

that the messianic promises were fulfilled during
the time of the Second Temple. In the Talmud it
is mentioned in the name of a rabbi Hillel, but
Saadiah cites it anonymously as the opinion of
"certain scholars who call themselves Jews."[82] This
opinion is based on the false assumption that such
prophecies as that the sun and the moon shall not
go down (Isaiah 20:20) would only come to be if
the Jews would be obedient to God. But when they
sinned, their sovereignty ceased, and such promises
never came to be. In similar fashion, promises about
redemption were conditional, and during the time
of the Second Temple some of these promises were
fulfilled, others were not. On the basis of Scriptural
verses, Saadiah argues that the promises concerning
the redemption were absolute, not subject to
conditions. To be sure, certain promises made to
Moses were conditional, but others were absolute.
Promises concerning redemption were in the second
group. One such reason is that promises concerning
redemption were put on par with promises made
to Noah. Just as it was promised to Noah that
an all-embracing flood will never come to be, so
was it promised to Isaiah (54:9) that even if the
people were to sin, the redemption will come.
Similarly it has been stated that at the time of
redemption the people will no longer sin. From
this it follows that redemption is not dependent on
any condition, so that all the promises and miracles
will come to be.

Having argued against those who hold that the
redemption has occurred in the past, Saadiah offers
fifteen arguments in support of the thesis that the

redemption will take place in the future.[83] All of these show that the messianic promises have not yet been fulfilled. Five arguments are taken from Scripture, five from history, and five from personal observation. Arguments from Scripture show that according to a prophecy in the book of Ezekiel, all Israelites will be gathered in their land; yet according to a report in Nehemiah 7:66, only 42,360 returned from the Babylonian exile. Similarly, according to a prophecy in Isaiah 60:11, the gates of Jerusalem will be perpetually open, yet according to a report in Nehemiah 7:3, the gates of Jerusalem were shut at times during the period of the Second Temple.

Arguments from history show, Saadiah continues, that the prophecies concerning redemption were not fulfilled in the past.[84] According to Isaiah 11:15-16, the Nile was supposed to become dry in one place, the Euphrates in seven places, so that the people could walk across. This has not yet happened. Similarly, the Temple at the time of redemption was to be built in accordance with the description in Ezekiel 43:12, yet the Second Temple was built in accordance with the varying description in Leviticus. Again, Ezekiel (43:11) predicted that a spring will come forth from under the Temple which would grow into a large river that no one could cross, yet this not yet happened.

Arguments from observation also show that the redemption could not have happened in the past.[85] For example, according to Zechariah 14:9, in messianic times all people will acknowledge the unity of God, but at the present many people do not, remaining in error and unbelief. Again, in messianic times wars will cease, yet observation shows that present times are marked by violent fighting. Should someone argue that the prophecy speaks only about wars concerning religion excluding other wars, observation once again shows that contemporary wars are about religion.

The arguments against those Jews who hold that the messianic times had come during the time of the Second Temple apply equally to the beliefs of the Christians.[86] But one argument must be added to these. Unlike Saadiah, who believed that the prophecies of Daniel had their beginning at the time of the building of the Second Temple, the Christians believe that they had their beginning 135 years before this time. By a more elaborate argument, also based on the book of Daniel, Saadiah shows that the Christian messianic beliefs are based on faulty chronology. These arguments may be urged against the Christians in addition to refuting their beliefs concerning the abolition of the Laws of the Torah and their trinitarian beliefs, which Saadiah had argued against in earlier parts of his work.

The final eschatological issue that Saadiah addresses is that of reward and punishment in the World to Come.[87] Referring to an earlier discussion in which he shows that the World to Come will begin when the number of souls whose existence divine wisdom has decreed have been created, Saadiah first undertakes to show by rational arguments that the World to Come must exist. One such argument is based on the nature of human life here on earth. In this world, well-being is bound up with misfortune, happiness with hardship, pleasure with pain, and joy with sorrow. It is incompatible with God's wisdom, his omnipotence and, most of all, with his kindness toward his creatures that the restricted happiness existing in this world is the only goal that human beings can attain. Hence there must be another world in which unrestricted happiness can be attained. Similarly Saadiah argues, rather pessimistically, that man by nature desires to commit adultery, steal, brag, and commit vengeance by murder, but he is restrained by his reason from committing these acts. The subsequent feeling of sadness and depression requires compensation, and for this is required the World to Come.

Still another argument is based on the justice of God.[88] We see that here on earth human beings practice violence on one another. Acts of violence benefit the one who commits them and work to the detriment of the one who suffers. Then both die without redressing the injustice. Hence, divine justice requires that there be a world in which this injustice is redressed. One more argument is based on the observation that in this world righteous persons suffer, while evildoers prosper. Once again, divine justice requires that there be a world in which righteous persons are ultimately rewarded, while wicked persons are punished.

Having presented rational arguments for the existence of the World to Come, Saadiah next turns to Scriptural passages that require the existence of the World to Come.[89] Pointing to the examples of Isaac, Hananiah, Mishael, Azriah and Daniel, all of whom were prepared to give up their lives, Saadiah argues that they would not have done this had they

not been convinced that there is a World to Come
in which they would receive their reward.

Turning to the knotty question: why does
Scripture emphasize reward in this world rather
than in the World to Come, Saadiah provides two
answers.[90] One of these is, that since reward and
punishment in the World to Come is demonstrable
by rational argument, there was no need for
Scripture to discuss it at length. According to
the other, since at the time of the giving of the
Torah, the Jewish people had greater need both of
knowledge concerning the Holy Land toward which
they traveled and of the earthly effects of their
obedience or disobedience to God, the prophets
spoke at length of these. There was no need to
elaborate on events that would occur in the distant
future. One more argument, once again one based
on divine justice, is provided by the suffering
and the death of small children. Referring to the
death of the children of the Midianites and the
death of the children of the generation of the
flood and to the pain of other small children, he
concludes that

> logical necessity, therefore, demands that there
> exist after death a state in which they would
> obtain compensation for the pain suffered
> prior thereto.[91]

From biblical citations, Saadiah proceeds to
rabbinic sayings.[92] In these the references are more
explicit and the term World to Come (*'olam ha-ba*)

appears as a technical term. We read, for example, that this world is like a vestibule for the World to Come (Abot 4:16), or, again, that one hour of repentance and good deeds in this world are better than the life in the World to Come (Abot 4:17).

For a description of the nature of life in the World to Come, Saadiah turns to a well known rabbinic passage—much discussed in the literature—which states:

> In the World to Come there will be neither eating nor drinking, nor trade nor procreation. But the righteous will sit with their crowns on their heads and enjoy the splendor of the divine presence (Berakhot 17a).[93]

While Saadiah holds that the human body exists in the World to Come, the nature of its existence differs from its existence in this world. In the World to Come human beings will neither eat nor drink, there will be no fatigue nor procreation, but the righteous will bask in the light of the divine presence.

Having shown that reward and punishment in the World to Come are given to the combined body and soul, Saadiah goes on to explain further the nature of these states.[94] Basing himself on a passage in the prophet Malachi (3:19-21), Saadiah explains that on the day of retribution God will create a very fine substance which will affect the righteous and the sinners in accordance with their desert. This substance will be like luminous fire. It will provide light for the righteous, but will burn the wicked. It is likened to the sun which both burns and provides light. There is, however, this difference between the new substance and the sun, that in case of the sun light and burning are inseparably intertwined, while, through the grace of God, they are separated in the new substance.

To explain how in the World to Come the human body can survive without eating and drinking, Saadiah points to the example of Moses, often cited in this context.[95] The bible relates three times how Moses lived for forty days and forty nights without eating or drinking, thereby providing evidence that human beings can live without food or drink. As one can learn from the verse "And Moses knew not that the skin of his face sent forth beams" (Exodus 34:29) that Moses was nourished by light, so can one learn that in the World to Come those who deserve it will also be nourished by light.

Since in the World to Come human beings will have bodies, there must exist in it place and time.[96] But the place must be a very special place described by Scripture as a "new heaven" and a "new earth" (Isaiah 66:22). The new earth is necessary because life in the World to Come will be different from life in this world. For in this world human beings eat and drink, so that fields and orchards, rivers and streams are required. But since in the World to Come there is neither eating or drinking, in the World to Come none of these are required. To describe further the difference between this world and the World to Come, Saadiah invokes a rather interesting argument from biology. In this world the air existing between the earth and the heavens extracts elements from our bodies which have to be replaced by food. But since in the World to Come there is neither eating nor drinking, no such air is required. Hence, the World to Come must be different from the world in which we live now.

Just as place is different in the World to Come, so is time.[97] In this world the distinction between day and night is required so that people can alternate between work and rest. Since in the World to Come there is no work and rest, in the World to Come there will only be light. Similarly time will not be divided into months and years, since fixed times are required for computing wages or for sowing and reaping. The only time that is required is one determining when divine worship is to take place.

Invoking arguments based on reason, Saadiah inquires about the length of time for reward and punishment in the World to Come.[98] He comes to the conclusion that both must be infinite. Since God required that human beings worship him, he must have implanted within them a desire for such service. Were the reward for service a limited time, say a thousand or two thousand years, a human being might say that this is not a strong enough incentive to worship God. If, however, the reward is infinite and unending, no room is left for such excuse. Concerning punishment, one might argue that eternal punishment would be an act of cruelty on the part of God. But turning to an argument similar to that offered for the case of reward, Saadiah argues that were punishment limited, human beings might not turn away from sin. For were punishment

limited in time, say one or two thousand years, a
sinner might argue that this is not enough deterrent
to keep him from sin. Eternal punishment is,
therefore, an act of kindness on the part of God,
since it provides the strongest possible deterrent
against sinning.

While reward and punishment in the World
to Come will be unending, still there will be
gradations.[99] This becomes clear through an analogy
with this world. Just as in this world there are people
whose happiness consists in being at rest, others
become happy through eating and drinking, still
others enjoy a good shelter, still others fine clothes
and, finally, others who in addition to all these
enjoy receiving honors, so, in the World to Come,
there are gradations in the reception of the light
of the divine presence. For some the light will be
like the sun rays in the morning, some additionally
will enjoy the warmth of the sun's rays, until the
highest reward will be to see the light as one sees the
clarity of the sun. Once again invoking an analogy
to human torment and pain, Saadiah describes the
punishment of sinners by seven destructive qualities
possessed by fire.

Those who suffer eternal punishment are divided
into three groups: unbelievers, polytheists, and
those who have committed grave sins of which they
have never repented.[100] For the latter group, death
at the hand of an earthly court has been prescribed.
Since they have been cut off from the righteous
by judicial decree in this world, argues Saadiah,
they will also be cut off from the righteous in the
World to Come. While those who have committed

minor sins and have repented will be forgiven, even those who have committed minor sins but have not repented will be forgiven as well. The very fact that they did not commit major sins provides evidence that they have resisted the temptation to commit major sins. While these will inherit the World to Come, they will be punished for their transgressions in this world.

Just as in this world human beings are obligated to render service to God, so are they obligated in the World to Come to render service to him.[101] They will be obligated to acknowledge his sovereignty, not to ascribe unworthy attributes to him, and to observe other duties of a rational nature. But in addition to these there will be designated places for worship in a manner to be determined at the time. In return for this service, the happiness of those who worship God will be increased. While, in a general way, we know the nature of the reward and punishment in the World to Come, we do not know the details of reward and punishment for the observance or neglect of every commandment and tradition. These details will be spelled out at the time of the redemption.

Ibn Gabirol and Maimonides

It seems strange, at first glance, that Naḥmanides should group Ibn Gabirol's and Maimonides' eschatological teachings together. For, Ibn Gabirol in his philosophic orientation follows the Neo-Platonic tradition, while Maimonides follows that of the Aristotelians. But the two have in common that they base their conception of the World to Come on psychological consideration and that they are more interested in the World to Come than in other eschatological notions.

Ibn Gabirol, the Avicebron or Avicebrol of the Latins, is known in medieval Christian philosophy through his *Fons vitae*, the original Arabic text of which has been lost, but in the Jewish world he was known as a pre-eminent Hebrew poet. As such he composed *The Kingly Crown* (*Keter Malkhut*) which became a part of the liturgy of the day of atonement. It was incorporated into this liturgy because the last eight stanzas contain a poetic version of the confession of sins—confession of sins being the theme of the day. But the philosophic sections which form a kind of philosophic preface to the liturgical conclusion have as their major theme the exalted nature of God and the low status of man. As means toward this end, Ibn Gabirol describes the origin of the world, its structure, the role of man within the world, and he develops these themes along Neo-Platonic lines intermingled with Pseudo-Empedoclean notions. While we have no firm evidence of Ibn Gabirol's sources, it is clear that his orientation and, with it, his conception of the World to Come is Neo-Platonic.[102]

The *Kingly Crown* begins with a description of the attributes of God which in typical Neo-Platonic fashion are interpreted as negations. For example, affirming the unity of God, Ibn Gabirol writes:

> ...Thou art One, and at the mystery of Thy
>   Oneness the wise of heart are astonished,
>   for they know not what it is.
> Thou art One, and Thy Oneness neither
>   diminishes nor increases, neither lacks
>   nor exceeds.
> Thou art One, but not as the One that is counted
>   or owned, for number and change cannot
>   reach Thee, nor attribute, nor form....[103]

From God, called the uppermost light (*'or 'elyon*), emanates, first of all, Wisdom (*ḥokhmah*), and from Wisdom emanates Will (*ḥefez*).[104] In order to safeguard the voluntaristic nature of emanation, Ibn Gabirol posits Will as a separate hypostasis. For the next emanation he turns to the Pseudo-Empedoclean notion of matter and form. Whereas for the Aristotelians it is form that determines the nature of a substance, for Pseudo-Empedocles it is matter. Hence, in accordance with this changed understanding of matter and form, everything below Will is composed of matter and form—even angelic beings and intelligences. In Ibn Gabirol's scheme, then, Will is followed by universal form (*sod*) and universal matter (*yesod*). Turning to religious terminology, Ibn Gabirol identifies the realm of universal matter and universal form with the Divine Throne (*kissei ha-kabod*). Next follow the cosmic intellect, the outermost sphere which is responsible for the daily rotation of the heavens, the remaining celestial spheres, the earth, and finally the four elements. It should be noted that whereas for Aristotle the cosmic intellect, known as the agent intellect, is the lowest of the celestial intelligences, for Ibn Gabirol it is the highest.

It is within this cosmological scheme that Ibn Gabirol places his eschatology. The cosmic intellect, described by him as the resting place of the righteous, is identified by Ibn Gabirol with the World to Come in which they receive their reward. In a stanza from which Naḥmanides extracts the quotation cited at the beginning of this volume, Ibn Gabirol writes:

> Who can do as your deed when you made
>   under the Throne of Thy Glory [the realm
>   of universal matter and universal form] a
>   place for the souls [that is, intellects] of
>   your righteous ones?
> There is the abode of the pure souls, that are
>   bound in the bundle of life.
> Those who are tired and weary, there will they
>   restore their strength.
> There shall the weary be at rest, for they are
>   deserving of repose.
> In it there is delight without end or limitation,
>   for that is the World to Come.[105]

From Ibn Gabirol's description it is clear that the immortality he envisages is incorporeal and individual, and it is equally clear that he does not believe in the possibility of mystical union with God. Less clear is his conception of the punishment of the wicked. The upper world is also the realm of their punishment, and in accordance with the severity of their transgression, they are punished by fire, rivers of sulphur, deep pits, storms, hail, ice, snow, heat, darkness and gloom. Having poetically described the "treasures" (*ozrot*) of those who are righteous and of repentant sinners, Ibn Gabirol continues describing the punishment of the sinners:

> ...Some of them [are] treasures of fire and rivers of sulphur, for the transgressors of the covenant,
> And treasures of deep pits of unquenchable fire, 'he that is abhorred of the Lord shall fall therein.'
> And treasures of storms and tempests, of freezing and frost,
> And treasures of hail and ice and snow, drought and also heat and bursting floods,
> Steam and rime and mist and cloud and darkness and gloom.
> All of them didst Thou prepare, in their time, either for mercy or for judgment Thou didst ordain them, 'O mighty God, Thou hast established them for correction'.[106]

From the cosmic intellect, the highest of the intelligences, there emanate angelic beings and the human soul, which has the power of understanding. Through the power of understanding and through the acquisition of knowledge, the soul can free itself from the body and acquire immortality. We are then in the presence of the typical Neo-Platonic scheme describing the descent of the human soul into the body and its ascent through the acquisition of knowledge to the cosmic intellect from which it came. Nothing can be learned from the *Kingly Crown* about Ibn Gabirol's beliefs concerning messianic times and resurrection since these topics fall outside the poem's theme.

Another description of Ibn Gabirol's cosmogony and eschatology can be found in his *Fons vitae*. While the five tractates of the work are devoted to a discussion of the various meanings of matter and form, some incidental remarks in the first and fifth tractate refer to the notions mentioned. Ibn Gabirol's emanationist scheme in the *Fons Vitae* parallels that set down in the *Kingly Crown*, though the relation of wisdom (*sapientia*) and will (*voluntas*) in the *Fons vitae* is less clear. Cast in a dialogue between a teacher and a student, the student asks in an early part of the work concerning the purpose of human life. The teacher answers:

> [The purpose of human life is] the attachment of the human soul to the upper world. By means of this everything returns to that which it resembles.[107]

To the student's further question of how this is attained, the teacher replies:

> Through knowledge (*scientia*) and action (*opus*), since through these [two] the soul is attached to the upper world. Knowledge brings to

action, and action removes the soul from those things opposite to it which damage it, thereby returning [the soul] to its nature and substance. In sum, knowledge and action free the soul from its enslavement to nature and purify it from its shadows and darkness. Thereby the soul returns to the upper world.[108]

In this cryptic passage, Ibn Gabirol describes the typical Neo-Platonic scheme of the descent of the soul from the upper world, more precisely from the cosmic intellect, and its return to it by means of knowledge and action. Since the *Fons vitae* is a philosophic book, he seems to refer to a kind of ascetic ethics which frees the soul from the hindrances of the body. How this ethics is related to religious commandments is not discussed.

The teacher next instructs the student in the essence of the soul and its nature, explaining that it is the soul's task to know all things as they are, especially to acquire knowledge of the first essence, the cause which sustains and moves all things. The student then asks whether it is possible to know the first essence. The teacher replies:

It is impossible to know the essence of the first essence (*essentia essentiae primae*) [as it is in itself]…, it is only possible to know it [the first essence] through its works (*opera*).[109]

While Ibn Gabirol does not spell out the nature of
this knowledge, it is reasonable to assume that he
has in mind the same kind of knowledge of God
through negation that he describes more fully in his
Kingly Crown. As reason for his view he states that
the first essence is infinite and the human mind can
only know something finite.

Pursuing the nature of human understanding
further, Ibn Gabirol maintains that three things are
to be known in the upper world: universal matter
and universal form, Will, and the first essence.
Having shown the limitation of knowing the first
essence, he states that it is also difficult to know the
nature of Will. To the student's question about the
nature of Will, the teacher replies:

> It is impossible to describe the Will, one can
> only describe it approximately by saying that
> it is a divine power which created [that is,
> emanated] universal matter and universal form
> and which combined them. It is spread out
> from the highest being to the lowest as the soul
> is spread throughout the body. And this power
> moves and orders all things.[110]

To the student's further question concerning the
nature of the Will, Ibn Gabirol replies that he has
written a book about the Will and urges the student
to read it after he has completed the *Fons vitae*.[111]
He even gives the title of the book, *The Source
of Emanation and the Cause of Generation* (*origo*

largitatis et causa essendi), but the book is not extant. It is not clear that Ibn Gabirol ever wrote it.

Ibn Gabirol returns to the eschatological notion of immortality at the end of his book. To the student's question concerning the use of acquiring knowledge, the teacher replies: "deliverance from death and attachment to the fountain of life [the cosmic intellect]."[112] The knowledge whereby immortality is achieved begins with knowledge of the world including the heavens, proceeds to knowledge of the cosmic intellect, and ends in knowledge of Will and the first essence, to the extent that knowledge of the last two is possible.

One more point in Ibn Gabirol's cosmology should be mentioned, and that is the respective place of Wisdom and Will in the emanationist scheme. In the *Kingly Crown*, which is devoted to a rather full description of this scheme, Wisdom and Will are separate hypostases, while in the *Fons vitae* they are sometimes combined into one.[113] In the *Fons vitae* he also sometimes mentions Will without discussing Wisdom. I do not believe that this marks a change in Ibn Gabirol's view. Since in *Fons vitae* he is primarily concerned with the various kinds of matter and form, and since Will is the immediate principle from which emanate universal matter and universal form, there is no need to mention Wisdom. Hence I attach no special significance in his combining the two. Similarly, I see no need to hold that in the *Kingly Crown* he proposes a voluntaristic emanationism, whereas in *Fons vitae* he proposes one that is necessary. After all, the latter mentions Will as the hypostasis between the

first essence and universal matter and form, and
not Wisdom.

With Moses Maimonides (1138-1204) the
discussion of eschatological doctrines shifts into
an Aristotelian psychological scheme. While Maimonides discusses the resurrection of the dead, the
Messiah and messianic times, and even the Garden
of Eden, Gehinnom, and the War of Gog and
Magog, the emphasis is on the World to Come.

That, according to Maimonides, there still existed
confusion about eschatological matters in his time
becomes clear from the discussion in chapter 10 of
the Treatise Sanhedrin in his *Commentary on the
Mishnah*. Referring to the widely differing opinions
among rabbinic Sages concerning these matters, he
writes in rather hyperbolic fashion:

> So much confusion has invaded their opinions
> that it almost impossible to find anyone whose
> opinion is uncontaminated by error.[114]

He goes on to list five such opinions, all of which
he rejects.[115]

One group believes that the ultimate reward
comes in the Garden of Eden. This is a place in
which people secure food and drink without efforts,
houses are made of precious stones, beds are covered
with sheets of silk, and rivers flow with wine and
fragrant oils. These also believe that Gehinnom is
the place of punishment for sinners. It is a place
of raging fires in which bodies are burned and in
which sinners suffer all kinds of afflictions. They

base their elaborate description on the words of the rabbinic Sages and passages in Scripture. Their error comes from understanding such passages in literal fashion.

A second group believes that the righteous will be rewarded in the Days of the Messiah. At that time men will be angels and they will live forever. They will grow in number and stature until they have occupied the whole world. These also believe that in the Days of the Messiah the earth will bring forth woven garments, baked bread, etc. The punishment of sinners is that they will not be alive in those days and will not participate in the reward of the righteous. The arguments of this group are also based on the literal reading of rabbinic sayings and biblical passages.

A third group believes that reward and punishment occur at the time of the resurrection of the dead. The righteous who are resurrected will return to their families and will live forever. The punishment of sinners is that they will not be resurrected. This opinion is also based on the literal reading of rabbinic sages and of passages in the bible.

A fourth group does not have one of the traditional terms for its eschatology but it describes the reward of those who fulfill the commandments as bodily peace, worldly success, fertile lands, many children, health, peace, and security. There will be an earthly king who will not only rule over Jews but over gentiles as well. The punishment of the sinners is vaguely described as not participating in these pleasures. Again, the literal reading of rabbinic sayings and biblical verses leads to this faulty opinion.

A fifth group, and this is the largest, combine these eschatological notions. They believe that the Messiah will come, that he will resurrect the dead, that those resurrected will enter the Garden of Eden, where they will eat and drink, living in perfect health forever. In this section Maimonides mentions nothing concerning the punishment of sinners. Having presented the five opinions current in his day, Maimonides concludes this phase of the discussion by holding that the major eschatological notion, that of the World to Come, is absent from all of them. More than that, he criticizes his contemporaries for being busy with such issues as how will the dead be resurrected. Will they be naked or will they be dressed, if they are dressed will they be dressed in the shroud with which they are buried or will they be dressed in an elaborate shroud? Concerning messianic times, they asked whether there will be rich and poor, weak and strong, and other questions of the same kind. While Saadiah, as we have seen, is occupied with such questions, it is clear from the tenor of Maimonides' discussion that he puts little stock in them.

Maimonides' own discussion is based on the three eschatological notions: resurrection of the dead, the Messiah and messianic times, and the World to Come. Of these he is primarily concerned with the World to Come. He discusses the resurrection of the dead and messianic times in his halakhic (legal) writings, but not in his *Guide of the Perplexed*. The reason seems to be that since the latter two principles are historical, they have no place in his *Guide*, a work devoted primarily to philosophic topics.

He mentions the resurrection of the dead in his *Commentary on the Mishnah*, where he lists it among the thirteen principles which every Jew is required to believe. It is interesting that he describes the origin of this principle to Moses. Tersely, he writes:

> The resurrection of the dead is one of the cardinal principles established by Moses our Teacher. A person who does not believe in this principle has no real religion, certainly not Judaism.[116]

Citing a statement in *Bereshit Rabba* which reads in part, "…the resurrection of the dead is only for the righteous," he goes on to affirm that resurrection is reserved only for these. Rejecting the rather fanciful description of what happens to sinners after death that some of his predecessors and contemporaries had proposed, he simply states that sinners will not be resurrected, that is, they will cease to exist. Citing in support of this opinion the rabbinic saying that sinners are "dead" even while still alive (Berakhot 18b), he asks if they are already dead in this life, how can they be resurrected? Maimonides lists the principle a second time in his *Mishneh Torah,* Laws of Repentance, where he classifies someone who denies the resurrection of the dead among those who have no part in the World to Come.[117]

Maimonides' limited mention of the resurrection of the dead became the subject of controversy already in his own time. To combat the notion that he did not believe in resurrection, he wrote his *Treatise on the Resurrection of the Dead*. There he reports that a student in Damascus denied the resurrection of the dead by citing Maimonides' *Mishneh Torah*.[118] Since this was an isolated case, Maimonides saw no need to address the issue. Next he received a letter from Yemen which stated that there were persons denying the resurrection of the dead, basing themselves on Maimonides' emphasis on the World to Come. This time Maimonides replied, reaffirming that resurrection is one of the "fundamental principles" of the Torah and that it precedes the World to Come. The controversy came to a head when Samuel ben Ali, the head of the yeshivah in Baghdad, wrote a treatise entitled *Treatise on the Resurrection of the Dead*. Learning first from letters of this treatise, Maimonides afterwards received the treatise itself. Noting that the treatise consisted of sermons and parables, Maimonides argues that these cannot be taken literally, but must be interpreted correctly. Moreover, Samuel is mistaken in taking the opinions of the Mutakallimûn as the correct opinions of the philosophers. And finally, Samuel used two philosophically defective books, the *Treatise on Reward* by Avicenna and the Mu'tabar.

Having set down his critique of Samuel, Maimonides reiterates his literal belief in the resurrection of the dead, which he had presented in his *Commentary on the Mishnah* and in his *Mishneh*

Torah. The belief is stated many times in prayers, prophetic writings, and rabbinic sayings, and there is no controversy concerning it among the Jewish people. Those resurrected, continues Maimonides, will eat and drink, have sexual relations and will produce children, and will die after a long life. In the World to Come, however, and this is the world of the real reward, the souls will exist without bodies. Arguing against those who believe that there exist rational arguments for the resurrection of the dead, Maimonides maintains that no such arguments exist and that the principle must be accepted, like other miracles, on the basis of reliable tradition alone. To be sure, the literal belief in the resurrection does not fit readily into his philosophic scheme, but I see no reason to classify him with such Muslim philosophers as Avicenna who consider the principle as a concession to the imagination of the masses who can only conceive of the existence of corporeal substances.

Similarly, Maimonides' discussion of the Messiah and messianic times is rather brief and limited to his halakhic (legal) works. His general tendency is to rid the doctrine of supernatural and apocalyptic elements. In messianic times, he states in his *Commentary on the Mishnah*, sovereignty will be restored to Israel and the Jews will return to their own land.[119] The reputation of the Messiah, a great king, will spread throughout the world and all nations will make peace with him. Those who oppose him will be destroyed.

Maimonides approvingly quotes the rabbinic saying that "the only difference between this world and the days of the Messiah is that oppression by other kingdoms will cease." In messianic times there will be rich and poor, strong and weak, and the order of nature will remain unchanged. Statements such as that in the future rivers will flow with wine and precious oils, that the earth will bring forth woven garments and baked bread cannot be taken literally but are metaphors for the ease with which necessities of life will be secured in messianic times. After a long life the Messiah will die and will be succeeded by his son and grandson. Human life will be longer since in messianic times there will be no troubles and worries.

Messianic times are not desired, as some confused people think, so that productivity and wealth may be increased, that men may ride on horses and drink wine to the accompaniment of song. Rather, these times are desired so that wisdom and goodness will prevail. All the commandments of the Law of Moses will once again be fulfilled and people will observe them of their own free will.

Incidentally, Maimonides considers two minor eschatological notions in his *Commentary*, but they seem rather unimportant to him.[120] The Garden of Eden is a fertile place here on earth containing the best resources, many rivers, and herbs that are pleasanter and sweeter than the ones we know now. God will disclose the road to it at a future time and man will be happy in it. Gehinnom is not the name of a place at all. It is a term referring to the punishment of the sinners. But no specific description of it is contained in the Talmud. Basing themselves on a statement by the prophet

Malachi (3:19), some maintain that at a future time the sun will come close to the earth and burn the wicked. Others, basing themselves on Isaiah (33:11), maintain that the punishment consists of a fire within their bodies that will consume the sinners.

Maimonides returns once again to the Messiah and messianic times, this time in *Mishneh Torah*, Laws of Kings and Their Wars.[121] The discussion is somewhat more extensive and more structured, but his attitude is the same. He writes:

> The king Messiah will arise and restore the kingdom of David to its former state and original sovereignty. He will rebuild the Sanctuary and gather the dispersed of Israel. All the ancient laws will be reinstituted in his days; sacrifices will again be offered; the Sabbatical and Jubilee years will again be observed in accordance with the commandments set forth in the Law.[122]

As others before him, he insists that the coming of the Messiah is not only predicted by the prophets, but it is already mentioned in the Law of Moses.

Reaffirming his naturalistic stance, Maimonides states once again that the Messiah will not have to perform miracles, bring anything new into being, or revive the dead. Proof is provided by the fact that Rabbi Akiba, a great teacher of the Law, and the scholars of his generation supported the failed Messiah, Bar Kozba (Bar Kokhbah), and they did

not ask him to perform any miracles. In summary
fashion Maimonides writes:

> Let no one think that in the days of the Messiah
> any of the laws of nature will be set aside, or any
> innovation be introduced into creation. The
> world will follow its normal course.[123]

The centerpiece of Maimonides' eschatology is
the World to Come, and to explain it he turns to
philosophical psychology, especially the theory
of the intellect. Here it is rather striking that
while he accepts a number of Avicennian notions
in metaphysics, he adamantly rejects Avicenna's
psychology. In fact the only time he mentions
Avicenna by name (other than in the well known
letter to Samuel Ibn Tibbon) is in the *Treatise on
Resurrection* where he criticizes Avicenna's opinion
concerning the afterlife.[124] Under the influence of
Neo-Platonic ideas, Avicenna held that the human
soul is an individual substance which emanates from
the cosmic intellect and enters the human body.
As the result of the virtuous life and acquisition of
knowledge, the human soul returns to the upper
world from which it came. While the Avicennian
scheme provides an attractive explanation of the
afterlife, Maimonides rejects it because he considers
it philosophically unsound.

Maimonides never provides a full-fledged exposition of his psychological teachings even though
they are crucial for his discussion of such topics as
prophecy, providence, and immortality. Yet enough

of his ideas are scattered throughout his writings to permit a reasonably accurate reconstruction of his views. In fact, Alexander Altmann, in his seminal essay "Maimonides on the Intellect and Metaphysics" undertook such a reconstruction and he accomplished it with admirable success.[125]

Against Avicenna, who, as we have seen, is of the opinion that the human soul is an individual substance that enters the body from without, Maimonides maintains that the human intellect comes into being together with the human body at the birth of man. Following the Aristotelian commentator, Alexander of Aphrodisias, Maimonides affirms that the human intellect, like other faculties of the soul, starts as a corporeal predisposition (*isti'dâd hakhanah*).[126] It differs, however, from other faculties of the soul, such as sensation, imagination, and appetite, in that, if actualized, it can survive death and become immortal. By contrast, the other faculties, even if actualized, come to an end with the death of man.

Maimonides' conception of human cognition goes back to Aristotle as interpreted by his commentators. It has been noted that, according to Alexander's interpretation, the human intellect begins as a predisposition or potentiality and, like any potentiality, it requires an agent for its actualization. Aristotle had described this agent rather vaguely as "an intellect which is what it is in virtue of making all things." Interested primarily in the function of this intellect, Aristotle has little to say about its nature. But by the time of Maimonides it had become generally accepted

that this "making" intellect, known as the "agent
intellect," was identical with the lowest of the
celestial intelligences. Maimonides is somewhat
vague about the role of this intellect in human
cognition. He appears to be opposed to the Avicennian opinion that this intellect, under the right
conditions, deposits knowledge into the human
mind. Rather, the human mind receives knowledge
through its ability to abstract knowledge from
imaginative forms that ultimately go back to sense
perception.

Following the Hellenistic commentators on
Aristotle, Maimonides' Muslim predecessors had
distinguished between two stages of the actualized
human intellect: the intellect in actuality and the
acquired intellect. The former represents the human
intellect reflecting on the external world; the latter
represents the human intellect reflecting on its
own content. Maimonides mentions the acquired
intellect only in a few passages,[127] but generally
speaks of the intellect in actuality.[128] It appears
that he conflates the distinction between the two
intellects, stating that the intellect in actuality
is "that which remains of a human being after
death"[129] and that it is through the acquisition of
the intellectual virtues that "man acquires eternal
existence."[130]

One of the troublesome issues of Maimonides'
description of the World to Come is whether he
believes in individual or, as Ibn Bâjja and Averroes,
in collective immortality. In most passages he
speaks of "souls" or "intellects" (plural) which are
immortal, but in *Guide* 1:74(7) he approvingly cites

Ibn Bâjja, a proponent of collective immortality. In support of his opinion, Ibn Bâjja holds that the celestial intelligences are individuals and are distinguished from one another in that one is the cause of the other. By contrast no such causal dependence exists among the actualized human intellects: Zayd (Ruben in the Hebrew translation) is not the cause of Umar (Simon in the Hebrew). From the absence of the principle of causal dependence, it follows that in its immortal state there is only one intellect for all men. Here is what Maimonides writes:

> Now you know that regarding the things separate from matter—I mean those that are neither bodies nor forces in bodies, but intellects—there can be no thought of multiplicity of any mode whatever, except that some of them are the causes of the existence of the others and that thus there is a difference among them since one is the cause and the other the effect. However, what remains of Zayd is neither the cause nor the effect of what remains of Umar. Consequently all [surviving human intellects] are one in number as Abû Bakr Ibn al-Ṣâ'igh and others who were drawn into speaking of these obscure matters have made clear.[131]

Some medieval commentators, such as Samuel Ibn Tibbon and Moses of Narbonne, and Shlomo Pines[132] among the moderns, emphasizing the Ibn Bâjja passage in the *Guide*, concluded that Mai-

monides is a proponent of collective immortality,
that is, that all immortal human intellects are one.
Against this interpretation Alexander Altmann has
argued (I believe convincingly) that Maimonides
believed in individual immortality. To be sure,
causal dependence as principle of individuality does
not exists in human intellects, but still they have
a principle for being individual in their immortal
state. According to Altmann, a clue to Maimonides'
final position is found in his statement that "the
survival of the soul [intellect] consists in the
survival of the objects of its knowledge inasmuch
as the one [the soul] is identical with the other
[the intelligibles], as the competent among the
philosophers have maintained the explanation of
which would be out of place here for reasons of
length."[133] As Altmann interprets this passage, it
means that the 'thing that survives' is not only
the objects of knowledge, the intelligibles, but
also the subject of knowledge, the intellect. For
as Maimonides, following Aristotle, had explicitly
stated, in knowing, the act of knowing, the subject
that knows, and the object that is known are one.
Moreover, Maimonides had asserted that there
are "many gradations" in our knowledge of God,
and there are gradations in intellectual status in
providence and in prophecy. From these examples
Maimonides concludes that just as there are variations by means of which intellects are distinguished
in this life, so are there variations by which intellects
are distinguished, that is, individualized in the next
life. According to this interpretation, the World to

Come consists of incorporeal intellects which are not only immortal but also individual.

Maimonides' adherence to Alexander's notion that the material intellect begins as a corporeal "disposition" raises the even more fundamental question whether he is entitled to a theory of immortality at all. For it is a principle of Aristotelian physics that "whatever comes to be must pass away." But this principle, Maimonides replies, applies only to the world after it has been created, not necessarily to a world created by God's will. For whatever was created by God's will can exist eternally through the same will. Scriptural proof for this principle is also provided by the description of [God's] *throne of glory.* None of the Sages has stated that this *throne*, though created, will pass away. More than that, Scripture has stated explicitly that this *throne* will last forever. Drawing an analogy, Maimonides writes:

> The same applied to the souls of the virtuous; for, according to our opinion, they are created, but will never become non-existent.[134]

In sum, just as the world which had a beginning is eternal *a parte post*, so the human intellect which has a beginning can become eternal, that is, immortal, *a parte post* through the acquisition of knowledge.

Maimonides' psychological interpretation of the World to Come raises a question about his conception of reward and punishment in the hereafter.

While it can be seen that the human intellect which
has become immortal can experience joy, it is more
difficult to conceive of punishment which consists
of total annihilation. For, this belief goes against
the intuition that someone being punished must
exist and must be aware that he is being punished.
Against this objection Maimonides would probably
argue that punishment is an ontological state rather
than a category of psychology, so that the awareness
of being punished is not a necessary condition
for punishment.

The Garden of Eden and Gehinnom have virtu-
ally no role in Maimonides' eschatology. In his
Commentary on the Mishnah he describes the Garden
of Eden as a fertile place containing the choices of
the earth's resources, many rivers, and fruit-bearing
trees.[135] Its location is presently unknown, but God
will reveal the road to it at a future time. It is also
possible that many wonderful plants will be found
there. Again, demonstrating a kind of naturalistic
bend, Maimonides adds that paradise would be
possible even if it had not been mentioned in the
Torah. How much more certain is its existence since
it has been mentioned in the Torah.

Gehinnom, for Maimonides, is not a place but
the name for the pain and punishment that will
befall the wicked.[136] No specific description of it
is contained in the Talmud, and, judging from
Maimonides' description of the afterlife, it will
befall the wicked in this life. He states in the
name of an unnamed teacher that the punishment
consists of burning. This is based on the passage
from the prophet Malachi which we have met in

our discussion of Saadiah's view. From Maimonides' attributing this opinion to a single unnamed teacher, it is clear that he puts little value in it.

As Saadiah before him, Maimonides cites Rav's saying that in the World to Come there is neither eating nor drinking, neither procreation nor commerce, but the righteous will sit, their crowns on their heads and will enjoy the radiance of the divine presence (*shekhinah*). But whereas Saadiah uses this saying to establish how in the World to Come human beings can have a body, even though these physical activities are lacking, Maimonides uses it to demonstrate that in the World to Come human beings exist as incorporeal intellects. Invoking an argument from the correlation of bodily members with their function, Maimonides maintains that since there is neither eating nor drinking, nor any other bodily activity, it follows that there is no need for the body in the World to Come. "Their crowns on their heads," interprets Maimonides, "refers to the eternal existence of the intellect through the existence of the intelligibles in it;" "they will enjoy the radiance of the divine presence (*shekhinah*)" "refers to the joy that the intellect experiences through what it understands of the Creator."[137]

Moses ben Naḥman (Naḥmanides)

From the quotation appearing earlier in this volume it is clear that Naḥmanides wishes to develop his conception of the World to Come according to tradition (*ke-halakhah*). While his exposition is based largely on rabbinic sayings, he is not immune to philosophic questions. As his discussion shows, he had philosophic training and was a careful student of Maimonides' thought. While he differed with the philosophic description of the World to Come proposed by Ibn Gabirol and Maimonides, he would sometimes invoke a philosophic argument or at least a philosophic analogy to prove a point. Toward Maimonides, for whom he had a great respect, he had a two-fold strategy. Confronted by a difficult passage, he would at times explain that Maimonides did not express himself fully. In that case he would expand Maimonides' discussion to bring it in accord with his own opinion. But there were other times when, though respectful of Maimonides, he would reject his opinion altogether.

Naḥmanides does not spell out the basis of his discussion of the afterlife, but it is clear that he, like Saadiah, bases it on divine justice. This is evident from the title "*The Chapter of Reward*" (*sha'ar ha-gemul*) which is similar to Saadiah's "Concerning Reward and Punishment in the World to Come," the ninth treatise of Saadiah's work.

Unlike the predecessors we have mentioned, Naḥmanides displays a great interest in the fate of the soul immediately after death. To explain this fate he appeals to the notions of *Gan Eden* and *Gehinnom*—notions which had little or no interest for Saadiah, Ibn Gabirol, and Maimonides. Citing numerous rabbinic sayings, Naḥmanides maintains that *Gehinnom* is a vast subterranean space to which sinners go immediately after death.

Naḥmanides begins by summarizing the arguments of those who deny the existence of *Gehinnom* altogether.[138] To hold that punishment is meted out to the body is absurd, for the body, whether in the grave or embalmed, is like a stone, and how can a stone be punished? Punishment must then befall the soul alone. But this is also impossible since punishment can only befall something having physical properties, and the soul has none of these. This is demonstrated by the opinion that punishment is by fire and fire must act on a body. It only remains that excision (*karet*), that is, ceasing to exist, is the only punishment of the soul. Against this view, attributed to foreign opinions espoused by pseudo-philosophers and idol worshippers, Naḥmanides argues that it makes punishment independent of the severity of the sin. Since according to this opinion all sins are punished by excision, the punishment for a light sin is the same as that for a grave sin. This is absurd. Punishment is, then, for both body and soul, and it takes place in *Gehinnom*.

Citing numerous rabbinic sayings, Naḥmanides maintains that *Gehinnom* is a vast subterranean space to which sinners go immediately after death.[139] The vastness of *Gehinnom* is described in the rabbinic saying that the world is one sixtieth as large as the *Gan* (Garden), the *Gan* one sixtieth as large as *Eden,* and *Eden* a sixtieth as large as *Gehinnom.* One thus finds that, in comparison to *Gehinnom*, the entire world is like the lid of a pot.

One of the most interesting supports for the physical nature of *Gehinnom* is derived from a halakhic (legal) ruling prohibiting the heating of

food or drink on the Sabbath. The ruling states that
it is forbidden to place a dish in the hot springs of
Tiberias on the Sabbath, "since these hot springs
are the result of fire, for the waters pass near the
entrance of *Gehinnom*."[140] Turning against those
who would interpret these sayings, Naḥmanides
holds that the rabbinic sayings must be accepted
in accordance with their literal meaning since the
rabbis specified the location and dimensions of
Gehinnom and since they made use of the notion in
their practical legal decisions.

Having affirmed that *Gehinnom* is a physical
place, Naḥmanides turns to the existence of the soul
in it. It would appear at first glance that to exist
within *Gehinnom*, the soul would need a body that
has corporeal properties. But this cannot be since
the body that exists at the time of death lies in the
grave or is left behind embalmed. But neither can
the soul inhere in some other kind of body having
physical properties. Akin to angelic beings, the
human soul consists of a "pure and extremely subtle
spirit" (*ruaḥ zakah ve-dakah beyoter*).[141] Adding an
implicit critique of the Neo-Platonic view, which,
as we have seen, was defended by Ibn Gabirol, he
adds, in an aside, that the soul was given "through
the breath of God and did not come to be through
emanation (*hishtalshelut*)."

To explain how the soul can be in place yet lack
other corporeal properties, Naḥmanides invokes a
clever philosophic analogy. There are philosophers
(he has in mind Neo-Platonists) who maintain that
the soul, that is, the intellect, is an incorporeal
substance attached to the body in some fashion.

While this soul does not have other corporeal properties, it can be said to be in place. Evidence is provided by the fact that when a person moves from place to place, the soul, though incorporeal, moves with its body in an accidental motion. Further support for this explanation is found in no other source than Maimonides' *Guide* (2.2). Naḥmanides cites the following passage:

> When man is moved by his soul, which is his form, to go up from the basement of his house to the upper story, we say that his body moves directly, while the soul, the actual efficient cause of the motion, participates in it accidentally. Through the movement of the body from the basement to the upper story, the soul has likewise accompanied it to the upper story, and when no fresh impulse for the motion of the body is given by the soul, the body which has been set in motion by such impulse comes to rest and the accidental motion of the soul is discontinued.[142]

The philosophers have attempted to explain how an incorporeal being can influence one that is material, but they have not been very successful in their attempt. In the end, Naḥmanides follows the rabbinic tradition according to which the soul, while lacking other corporeal properties, can still be in place in *Gehinnom*.

Having described the soul and its punishment in *Gehinnom*, Naḥmanides returns to the punishment

of the soul known as "excision" (*karet*).[143] Here
he argues against the notion that "excision" in
the rabbinic literature refers exclusively to the
destruction of the soul. From a passage in the *Sifra*
it appears that "excision" refers to the destruction
of the soul. But this is not the case, for "excision"
is a term for a severe punishment. It is not like the
destruction of the souls of animals which return
to their corporeal elements. The punishment of
Gehinnom comes to the wicked immediately after
death. His soul is attached to the sphere of fire
and attached to the River of Fire which, issuing
from the Throne of Glory, descends into *Gehinnom*.
The punishment of *Gehinnom* consists in the soul's
realization that its sins keep it from rising to a
higher sphere. This punishment comes immediately
after death, not at the time of the Messiah, and lasts
for twelve months.

Excision as a form of punishment, continues
Naḥmanides, has several meanings.[144] For those
who have lived a good life but have sinned through
their passions, excision means premature death.
They are not deprived of the reward of the World
to Come. Then there are those whose sins exceed
their merits. These may sometimes lead a life of ease
and may even attain old age, but in the end they
are cut of from life in the Garden of Eden. Finally
there are severe sinners, who commit such grave
sins as worshipping idols or being heretics. These
suffer both kinds of punishment: their body is cut
off from life in this world, their soul is punished
in *Gehinnom* forever, and they have no share in
the World to Come.

Having presented his own view based on rabbinic tradition, Naḥmanides now turns to the opinion of Maimonides.[145] From words in *Mishneh Torah* it appears that Maimonides proposes destruction of the soul as the only form of punishment. But this cannot be Maimonides' true opinion, for this is like the opinion of the heretics. Maimonides, comments Naḥmanides, did not express himself sufficiently clearly. In these sections of *Mishneh Torah*, Maimonides refers to the severe sinner whose punishment is destruction of the soul. However, in another section of *Mishneh Torah* he writes:

> All wicked persons whose sins exceed their merits are judged according to their sins and have a portion in the World to Come, for all Israel have a portion in the World to Come. These are the ones who have no portion in the World to Come, but are cut off, perish, and are eternally punished in accordance with their great wickedness and sinfulness: the Sadducees [who deny the validity of the oral tradition], scoffers, deniers of the Torah, etc.

From this citation Naḥmanides infers that Maimonides distinguishes between those who are punished (in *Gehinnom* after death) and those whose soul is destroyed because of the severity of their sins.

There is, however, another passage which does not lend itself to interpretation, and here Naḥmanides holds that Maimonides is mistaken.[146] This passage, found in the *Commentary on the Mishnah*, reads:

> The great punishment of the wicked is the cessation and extirpation of the soul to the extent that nothing is left thereof. This is the purport of what is mentioned in the Torah on the subject of excision, as it is said 'that soul shall be utterly cut off (*hikareit tikareit*)....'

And in a subsequent passage Maimonides writes:

> However, *Gehinnom* is a substitute designation for the punishment of the wicked. It is not explained in the Talmud how this punishment will occur.

From Maimonides' explicit statement it follows that Maimonides believed that the judgment of sinners takes place immediately at the time of death and that this punishment consists of the excision of the soul, that is, its ceasing to exist. *Gehinnom*, for Maimonides, is simply another term for the non-existence of the soul.

Against Maimonides, Nahmanides argues that there is another time for the final judgment concerning the state of the soul.[147] This day of judgment will occur at the beginning of the messianic period when it will be decided who will be resurrected and enjoy life in the World to Come and who will not be resurrected but will suffer punishment that is eternal. From a number of Talmudic statements

Nahmanides draws the conclusion that there is a difference between *Gehinnom* which exists now and the day of final judgment, which comes at the beginning of messianic times.

Having discussed the punishment of evildoers after death, Nahmanides turns to the reward of the righteous after death.[148] The tradition describes these rewards as *Garden of Eden* and the *World to Come* (these rewards are supplementary to those of messianic times and the time of the resurrection). Just as existence in *Gehinnom* occurs to the wicked immediately after death, so does existence in the *Garden of Eden* occur for the righteous immediately after death. Of the many rabbinic sayings cited by Nahmanides, the following is typical:

> [The wicked justify the divine judgment by saying:] You (God) have judged well. It is well that you have prepared *Gehinnom* for the wicked and the *Garden of Eden* for the righteous (Chagigah 15a).

The *Garden of Eden* is a place here on earth from which four rivers issue forth and which is described in the Torah.[149] The biblical description of this place is confirmed by geographers, in ancient medical books, and in the book of Assaf the physician. Many travelers have reported that they have seen "the flaming sword that turns" of which the bible speaks. Yet while Nahmanides reiterates his belief in the existence of the *Garden of Eden* here on earth, he also affirms that the earthly garden alludes to secrets of the upper world.

While Naḥmanides describes the *Garden of Eden* as a place here on earth, the question arises, what reward can the souls receive after death?[150] Since these souls do not possess ordinary bodies, it appears that they cannot enjoy the bodily pleasures that exist here on earth. Naḥmanides replies that since the *Garden of Eden* also refers to the secrets of the upper world, those in the *Garden* experience those joys that come with an understanding of the secrets of the upper world. Referring to the spiritual meaning that, by analogy, is contained in the earthly *Garden of Eden*, Naḥmanides writes:

> In that honored place [the earthly *Garden of Eden*] He (God) designed the entire function of the higher world, the World of Souls, within a physical mode of creation, so that [man] would be able to understand therefrom the foundations of all creation—physical, spiritual, and angelic—and [the foundations] of all the [perceptive] power which these creations can [exert to] conceive of the creator.[151]

Naḥmanides summarizes:

> Thus in *the Garden of Eden*, which is the chosen place for understanding all the higher secrets through the imagery of things, the souls of the dwellers [therein] become elevated by that study and they perceive *visions of God*.[152]

In a somewhat different vein, Naḥmanides speaks of another existence of the soul after death.[153] This is based on the rabbinic saying that

> The souls of the righteous are hidden under the Throne of Glory, as it is said 'and the soul of my lord [David] shall be bound in the bundle of life with the Eternal thy God' (Shabbat 152b).

And in another rabbinic passage it is stated that the souls of the righteous exist in the Aravot, the seventh heaven.

To resolve this two-fold existence of the soul, Naḥmanides holds that even though souls after death do not have a body, they participate in earthly pleasures and at the same time the pleasures of the higher world.[154] To support this notion, Naḥmanides cites the saying:

> For twelve months after death the body exists and the soul ascends to the heavens and descends therefrom. After twelve months, the body disintegrates and the soul ascends to heaven and does not descend.

In stating that the body exists during the twelve months after death, the rabbis do not have in mind the body that exists in the grave or that which is embalmed, but rather that the pleasures in the *Garden of Eden* incline toward corporeal

pleasures. This does not mean that they enjoy the
pleasure of the fruits of the *Garden* or bathing in
its rivers but they derive a more spiritual pleasure
through realizing that the earthly *Garden* is *the
gate of heaven.*

Having discussed at length *Gehinnom* and the
Garden of Eden, Naḥmanides now turns to his
conception of the *World to Come*, the place of
the ultimate reward for those who observe the
commandments of the Torah.[155] Taking issue with
Maimonides who holds that this world exists now,
Naḥmanides argues that it will come to exist at a
future time, after the resurrection of the dead. This
meaning is supported by the language used. For it
is not said concerning those who merit the World
to Come that they exist in it, but rather that they
"merit" it or that they""are designated for life" in
it. The World to Come differs from the world of
the souls, also called the *Garden of Eden*, which
comes to the righteous immediately after death.
Naḥmanides describes the stages of the afterlife even
more explicitly when he writes:

> All these statements [of the Rabbis] clearly
> indicate that the World to Come, which is
> referred to in all these places, is not [synonymous
> with] the World of the Souls and the reward
> which reaches the deceased immediately after
> death. Rather it is the world which the Holy
> One, blessed be He, will create after the era
> of the Messiah and the resurrection of the
> dead.[156]

As his predecessors, Naḥmanides cites the saying of Rav that "in the World to Come there is no eating nor drinking ... (but) the righteous will sit with their crown upon their heads and they will delight in the Glory of the divine presence" (Berakhot 17a).[157] Unlike Maimonides, however, Naḥmanides provides a reading that is closer to the statement's literal meaning. Just as the soul's existence in the body in this world is sustained through eating and drinking, so man's existence in the World to Come is sustained by being nourished through the light of the divine glory.

That the soul in the World to Come will have a body is further shown by two much discussed biblical examples.[158] One of these is Elijah who ascended into heaven without having died. Thus his soul was not separated from his body. The other is Enoch of whom it is said "that he was not," which according to the rabbinic interpretation means that he ascended into heaven without having died. Rabbi Simon, expanding on these two examples, comments on the verse "whatever God doeth shall remain forever," saying that man, as created, was destined to live forever. It was only because he sinned that he and his descendants became subject to death.

Naḥmanides, having argued for the existence of bodies in the World to Come, goes on to state that the body of those who are pure of soul, that is the righteous, is composed of subtle things (*devarim dakim*), while the bodies of those who are still purer are composed of the most subtle things (*devarim dakim min ha-medakkim*).[159] Evidence of how the

body was supported by something coming from
the upper world is provided by the manna. For, the
manna which sustained the people in the desert
came from the upper light (*'or 'elyon*), which,
through the will of the creator, became bodily
(*mitgashem*). An even higher level was reached by
Moses, whose body was sustained by the Glory of
the divine presence.

Naḥmanides once more addresses the philosophic
conception of the afterlife which he opposes.[160]
According to the philosophers the human body
has three organic functions, all of which have
their separate organs: ingestion and digestion of
food, procreation, and well-balancing of the body.
More than that, according to the philosophers the
body exists for the consumption of food, which
permits the body to exist and to produce its like.
Since in the World to Come there is neither eating
nor drinking, there do not exist the body's goals.
Since God does not create anything in vain, the
philosophers conclude, no need for the body exists.
To be sure, Naḥmanides replies, there will be no
need for the lowly body composed of the elements,
but a need for a body still exists. This will be the
body that God will resurrect at the time of the
resurrection. The existence of the body at that
time will be like the existence of the soul which
will exist through the knowledge of the most high.
Naḥmanides concludes that while according to the
philosophers and the philosophic commentators on
the bible (he seems to have Maimonides in mind)
no body exists in the World to Come, our tradition

teaches us matters to which philosophers have no access. Naḥmanides writes:

> Although our philosophical knowledge can not [help us to] perceive in what way this will be accomplished, we nevertheless believe that it will be so, for the creator, blessed be His name, knows the secrets of the soul and its essence more than [we in] our attempt at wisdom.[161]

Having discussed the various arguments for his eschatological teachings, Naḥmanides summarizes his opinion as follows:

> The reward of the souls and their existence in the World of Souls is called *Gan Eden* by our rabbis. Occasionally they call it the "Upper Chamber" or the "Academy on High." After the World of Souls will come the era of the Messiah, which is part of this world. At the conclusion thereof the great judgment and the resurrection of the dead will occur. This is the recompense which includes the body and the soul. This is the great principle which is the hope of all who look longingly to the Holy One, blessed be He. It is the World to Come, in which the body will become like the soul and the soul will be cleaving to *the knowledge of the Most High*, just as it adhered to that knowledge in the *Gan Eden* of the World of Souls. Now, however, it will be elevated to an even higher degree of

perception than heretofore, and the existence
of all will be forever and ever.[162]

The last part of the discussion is devoted to a critical examination of Maimonides' opinion.[163] Naḥmanides begins by approvingly citing Maimonides'
words in the *Commentary on the Mishnah* which
state that "in the World to Come, our souls will
attain the secrets of the Creator just as or even
more than the stars and the spheres achieve those
secrets." Those inhabiting the World to Come will
delight in the Glory of the divine presence, that is
to say, they will delight in their knowledge of divine
secrets. Naḥmanides approvingly cites this statement
since it has already been mentioned in the words
of the rabbinic sages. The rabbis have designated
the position of the righteous as being under the
Throne of Glory, where their reward consists in
their knowledge of God. This knowledge, however,
is not of the essence of God, since the divine essence
is unknowable to man. But no man in this life
can know the essence and the goodness of the
World to Come, for this is known to God alone.
Maimonides writes:

> The ancient sages already informed us that no
> man has it in his power to perceive the essence
> and goodness of the World to Come, and no
> one knows its grandeur and beauty except for
> the Holy One, blessed be He.

The words of Maimonides, comments Naḥmanides, on the excellent and delightful nature of the World to Come "are correct."

Having cited Maimonides' description of the World to Come, Naḥmanides proceeds to his critique.[164] This is primarily based on a *responsum* in which Maimonides approvingly writes that the Greek and Western philosophers agree that the soul, after death, is an immaterial and incorporeal substance which is delighted by perceiving the eternal light which is the World to Come. Maimonides' description, according to Naḥmanides, is faulty on two points, in both of which it differs from tradition. First of all, according to Maimonides, the World to Come is the world of incorporeal souls. According to tradition, to which Naḥmanides subscribes, the body exists in some fashion in the World to Come. Then again, Maimonides believes that the World to Come exists now and that those worthy of it enter it immediately after death. By contrast, Naḥmanides holds that tradition teaches that upon death those worthy of it enter *Gan Eden*, and the World to Come does not come to be until after the time of the Messiah and the time of the last judgment. In addition to the *responsum* that has been cited, Naḥmanides confirms from explicit citations in *Mishneh Torah*, the *Commentary on the Mishnah*, and the *Treatise concerning the Resurrection of the Dead*, that it is indeed Maimonides' opinion that the World to Come exists now and that in it the souls that exist are incorporeal.

Levi ben Gershom (Gersonides)

Levi ben Gershom (1288-1344), also known as Gersonides, wrote his magnum opus *The Wars of the Lord* for scholars trained in "the mathematical sciences, the natural sciences, and metaphysics."[165] Unlike some of his predecessors, he presents his opinions in straightforward, technical, philosophic fashion. Invoking what has been described as the scholastic method, he presents different views on a given philosophic topic, then arguments for, as well as against each view, and finally his own opinion with arguments in its support. He also assures his reader that his philosophic views are in agreement with the opinions of the Torah.

Just as Gersonides endorses a rigorous philosophic method, so does he endorse an orderly and systematic exposition. Possibly having Maimonides in mind, he writes:

> ...we have not employed rhetorical flourishes or obscure language; the profundity of the subject, together with right organization and clear language, are sufficient. There is no need to add obscurity of language and bad organization.[166]

Proceeding to write on six topics which his predecessors—as Gersonides saw it—had discussed insufficiently or concerning which they had proposed theories that were false, Gersonides undertook to fill in the lacunae and to correct the mistakes that his predecessors had made.

Two philosophers dominated the philosophic climate of Gersonides' period: Maimonides, whose *Guide of the Perplexed* had become a standard work, and Averroes, thirty-six of whose thirty-eight commentaries on Aristotle's works had been translated from Arabic into Hebrew.[167] While both of these may be described as Aristotelians, Maimonides—at least in his metaphysics—inclined toward the more Neo-Platonically colored Aristotelianism of Avicenna, while Gersonides, in spite of reservations, inclined toward the more naturalistic interpretation proposed by Averroes.

Gersonides' opinion concerning human immortality, which for him consists in the survival of the acquired intellect (*ha-sekhel ha-niqneh*), ultimately goes back to Aristotle's discussion in the third book of the *De Anima*. In a passage, the obscurity of which has vexed the commentators, Aristotle describes the process of thinking as a philosopher of nature, not as a metaphysician. Hence he is more interested in thinking as a change or process than in the intellects as substances that think. Since, then, thinking is a kind of change, it must exhibit the four causes required to explain any kind of change. Of these, the material and efficient causes are the ones that primarily engage Aristotle's attention. Concerning these he writes at the beginning of *De Anima* 3.5:

> Since in every class of things, as in nature as a whole, we find two factors involved, (1) a matter which is potentially all the particulars included in the class; (2) a cause which is

productive in the sense that it makes them
all (the latter standing to the former as, for
example, an art to its material), these elements
must likewise be found within the soul [that,
is the intellect].[168]

What then are the characteristics of intellect as
the material cause of thinking? Drawing an analogy
between thinking and seeing, Aristotle holds that
this intellect must be impassible, that is, it must be
capable of receiving a form without being subject to
any change. It must be capable of receiving all forms
(as intelligible universals), it must be unmixed, that
is it cannot have any form of its own. The capacity
for thinking is its only nature. Similarly, it cannot
be intermingled [at least not directly] with the body
for, if it were, it would possess a determining quality
such as being hot or cold or it would possess some
corporeal organ. This intellect must be separable,
in some fashion, from the body, and, if separable,
it must be simple.

If thinking is like seeing, there must exist an
intelligible form that is in some sense an efficient
cause of thinking, just as there exists a visible form
which is the efficient cause of seeing. In *De Anima*
3.5 Aristotle does not consider this question, but in
De Anima 3.7 he writes: "…the faculty of thinking
then thinks the form in the images…."[169]

It is the intelligible form residing in the images,
which is the object of thought. It should be noted,
however, that the intelligible form residing in the

image is particular, while the intelligible existing in the intellect is universal.

The term "agent intellect" as a technical term was introduced by the commentator, Alexander of Aphrodisias. Aristotle, in *De Anima* 3.5 speaks more informally of an intellect which "is what it is by virtue of making all things." While Aristotle compares the function of this intellect to the role of light in seeing, it is less clear how he conceives of light. If, as it seems likely, he has in mind a light-producing cause, such as the sun or fire, the agent intellect would be an efficient cause of thinking, existing apart from the material intellect. This interpretation would seem to be supported by Aristotle's description of the agent intellect as "separable, impassible, unmixed, since it is in its essential nature activity." The agent intellect would then "illumine" the intelligible form residing in the image, making it possible for the material intellect to abstract the universal intelligible from the particular intelligible form residing in the image. Whatever Aristotle had in mind, it seems to be clear that he is not a proponent of some form of "infusionism" or "illuminationism" according to which the agent intellect deposits the intelligibles into the material intellect.

In a final passage of *De Anima* 3.5, Aristotle distinguishes between two kinds of knowledge: knowledge of intellect as such and knowledge of particular intellects. The knowledge of intellect as such is eternal; the knowledge of particular intellects is temporal. Yet in spite of their temporality, individual human intellects seem to be able to free themselves from their temporal, corporeal condition, thereby becoming "immortal and eternal."[170] Aristotle never explains what this immortal state may be or how it may be attained.

The Hellenistic commentators on Aristotle undertook to make Aristotle's rather vague theory of the intellect and thinking more precise and to present his views in more systematic fashion. Among these the two most important ones were Alexander of Aphrodisias (ca. 200 C.E.) and Themistius (ca. 320-ca. 390). Muslims came to know their opinions through Arabic translations of their works. The opinions of these two were reported and criticized by Averroes (1126-1198), who, in turn, presented his own opinions in his three commentaries on the *De Anima*—Epitome, Middle Commentary and Long Commentary. It is through the Hebrew translation of Averroes' Epitome and Middle Commentary that the opinions of these three commentators (as well as the opinions of Aristotle) reached Gersonides.

Since the intellect is that part of the soul that can become immortal, Gersonides devotes the first book of his *Wars* to a discussion of the nature of the intellect. Beginning with the material intellect (*ha-sekhel ha-hiyulani*), he discusses three (respectively four) theories that had been proposed concerning it. Since the human intellect exists together with the body and since it receives knowledge of universals by abstracting them from the images, it seems to follow that the material intellect must be corporeal in some way. But since the intelligibles that the intellect knows are universals, lacking corporeal properties, the material intellect must also be incorporeal. One further difficulty in the search for the immortality of the intellect is Aristotle's statement in *De Caelo* 1.12 that whatever is generated must cease to exist.

The first of the three opinions considered by Gersonides is that of Alexander of Aphrodisias.[171] Emphasizing the corporeal aspect of the material intellect—after all, it comes into being with the birth of man—this commentator identifies it as a disposition (*hakhanah*) the underlying subject of which is the imaginative faculty or the intelligible forms residing in the imagination. By contrast, Themistius, the proponent of the second view, emphasizing that the intelligibles existing in the human intellect are universals, maintains that this disposition must have as its subject an incorporeal intellect that neither comes to be nor ceases to exist. Striking a middle ground, Averroes maintains that this disposition is in one respect an incorporeal substance, in another respect a corporeal disposition. As an incorporeal substance the material intellect is identical with the agent intellect, as a disposition having the potentiality for knowing terrestrial phenomena it is attached to the imagination. To these three opinions Gersonides adds a fourth, that of unnamed Christian scholastics, according to which the material intellect is an incorporeal substance, but one that is generated essentially, not accidentally.

Having enumerated the four opinions concerning the material intellect, Gersonides offers a number of arguments for each opinion.[172] Of these the following are typical. In support of Alexander's opinion, it may be argued that since Aristotle calls this intellect a disposition, not a substance, it cannot be an incorporeal intellect, which is a substance. In support of Themistius' opinion it may be urged that were the material intellect a corporeal disposition, it could not understand universals, since a material faculty can only perceive particulars. Taking an intermediary position, Averroes borrows arguments both from Alexander and Themistius. From Alexander he borrows an argument derived from the fact that the human intellect is generated. When a human being is born, the agent intellect becomes a disposition in an individual human being, and when the human being dies, the individual human intellect ceases to exist. From Themistius he borrows an argument designed to show that the intellect is an incorporeal substance. The material intellect, as a corporeal disposition, comes to an end with the death of man, while the incorporeal intellect continues to exist. The fourth opinion, that of the Christian scholastics, can also be sustained by arguments taken from Alexander and Themistius.

Having presented arguments in support of the four theories concerning the material intellect, Gersonides goes on to consider their validity.[173] Since none of these arguments are contradictory, there is no way in which any one argument can be proved or disproved. The best that one can hope for is to refute any or all of the arguments offered in support of the four theories. If one has determined which of these theories is false, it will be easier to find a theory that is true. Alternately, if all of them are false, one can develop a new and different theory.

After presenting a number of arguments against each opinion,[174] Gersonides proceeds to his own view.[175] Since, as has been shown, the underlying subject of the material intellect cannot be an immaterial intellect, this subject must either be a soul or a body. It cannot be a soul since the soul is the form of the body and a body—as any subject—cannot receive two forms simultaneously (this has been shown in arguments against Themistius). It remains that the human body must be the subject for the material intellect.

The body, however, cannot be the subject of the material intellect in any simple fashion. For if it were, the actualized human intellect would cease to exist with the death of man. To remove this difficulty, Gersonides distinguishes between different kinds of receptivity. There is, first of all, the kind of receptivity in which that which it receives affects the subject. The hand becomes hot or cold by touching a hot or cold object. Then there is the kind of receptivity which, in one respect, is mixed with matter, but in another respect is not mixed. The latter takes place in the case of color. While the eye in perceiving color does not actually become colored, still, the visual percept is material. Finally, there is the case of the intelligibles, in which the intelligibles in actuality are not mixed with matter at all. For, while the material intellect is a disposition belonging to the imagination, the imagination serves *only* as a *subject* for this disposition. As subject the imagination receives the material intellect in a secondary way, so that this intellect does not take on any of the physical properties of the imagination.

This differs from the opinion of Alexander who thought that the imagination is not only the subject for the material intellect's existence but also for its act of cognition.

Having discussed the nature of the material intellect, Gersonides next turns to the agent intellect (*ha-sekhel ha-po'el*). By the time of Gersonides it was generally accepted that this intellect is the lowest of the incorporeal celestial intelligences, namely, that which governs the sub-lunar world. As such it is both the efficient cause of the orderly arrangement of this world as well as an efficient cause in thinking. As efficient cause of this order, the agent intellect "possesses complete knowledge [of the sub-lunar world]."[176] By contrast, the human intellect, depending for its knowledge on sense perception, apprehends this knowledge in a "diffuse and disordered way."[177]

In order to explain the agent intellect's role in knowing, Gersonides rejects two interpretations of Aristotle's light analogy.[178] According to one of these, the agent intellect transforms the intelligible form residing in the imagination into an actual object of knowledge. But there is no way in which a particular can be transformed into a universal. Nor can the agent intellect endow the material intellect with a power enabling it to apprehend the universal intelligible in the image. For if it did, the material intellect would understand all the features of the image, including those that make for its particularity, such as a particular color or a particular shape, and this is not possible.

Having disposed of two interpretations of Aristotle's light analogy, Gersonides turns to his own interpretation of the role of the agent intellect in the production of human knowledge.[179] This description, in my view, may be considered another interpretation of the light analogy. Stimulated by the images in the imagination—which are based on sense perceptions of the sub-lunar world—the agent intellect deposits intelligibles into the material intellect. It appears to me that, thereby, Gersonides accepts a kind of "infusionism" or "illuminationism" as the theory of how the human intellect knows.

But there are two objections to Gersonides' thesis.[180] If human knowledge is derived from images that ultimately go back to the sub-lunar world, how can the intellect know the practical arts, mathematics, the heavenly bodies and their movers, and the first mover—all of which have no images corresponding to them? The second objection is: if human knowledge is imparted by the agent intellect which contains all knowledge, why is it that human knowledge is partial and that human beings differ in the knowledge they possess?

In answer to the first objection it may be stated that it is true that while human beings possess full knowledge only of sub-lunar phenomena, they do possess some knowledge of mathematics, the celestial bodies and their mover, and, especially, the first cause. But this knowledge is partial and inferior. For, these the human intellect knows not directly, as it knows the sub-lunar world, but indirectly as causes having effects in this world. Cause and effect are relational terms, and knowledge of effects produces knowledge of causes.

To dispose of the second objection, namely, that human knowledge is imperfect compared to the knowledge of the agent intellect, Gersonides states that since knowledge of the sub-lunar world depends on sense perception, and since sense data are uneven, there is a difference in knowledge even of the sub-lunar world.

Gersonides finally discusses the primary subject of book one of the *Wars*—human immortality. Turning to his predecessors, he considers three opinions, all of which he rejects.[181] The first of these is that of Alexander, Themistius, and Averroes. According to these, the material intellect cannot become immortal insofar as it understands the sub-lunar world, for, whatever exists in this world comes to be and ceases to exist. By contrast, the incorporeal intelligences, especially the agent intellect, are eternal, and it is only through "being united" (*she-yit'ahed*) with the agent intellect that the human intellect can become immortal. As Gersonides states: "In apprehending the agent intellect the material intellect becomes immortal."[182] While it is clear to me that this is the opinion of Averroes, it is less clear to me why Gersonides ascribes this opinion to Alexander and Themistius.

The second opinion is that of Avicenna.[183] According to this philosopher it is the acquired intellect that is immortal. Since the material intellect is an incorporeal substance and, hence, immortal, and since the intelligibles, the objects of knowledge existing in the agent intellect, are also immortal, it follows that the acquired intellect is immortal.

Alfarabi has two opinions. According to the *Commentary on the Nicomachean Ethics* [now lost], he denies human immortality altogether. According to his *Letter concerning the Intellect*, he describes human immortality in a way similar to Themistius. Calling the actualized human intellect the "acquired intellect," he states that this intellect can become immortal by conceiving the agent intellect.

Having presented arguments for and against these three opinions,[184] Gersonides presents his own interpretation of the acquired intellect and with it, his theory of human immortality.[185] The discussion is governed by two principles. According to one of these, the intelligibles, that is, the objects of knowledge, are generated in the material intellect. According to the other, the acquired intellect is immortal.[186]

The acquired intellect is the perfection of the material intellect produced by the agent intellect. This perfection occurs in two ways: through conception (*ẓiyyur*) and through judgment (*ha-'amatah*). Conception consists of knowledge of the universal intelligibles as they exist in the agent intellect, and the acquired intellect knows the intelligibles as they exist in that intellect. Hence, just as the intelligibles in the agent intellect are eternal, so those existing in the acquired intellect are eternal *a parte post*, that is, the acquired intellect is immortal. But even knowledge based on judgments is eternal. For since it is true that such judgments as "all animals have sensation" (this is Gersonides' example) are derived from images based on sense perception as well as intelligibles in the agent intellect, it follows that even judgments exist in the agent intellect. Gersonides concludes that the human intellect is immortal through both conception and judgment. But since knowledge of any kind goes back to sense perception, no new knowledge can be acquired by human beings after death.

To rebut the opinion of Alexander, Themistius, and Averroes, Gersonides shows that it is impossible that the human intellect should become one with the agent intellect.[187] For were this the case, the acquired intellect would have to possess all the knowledge inhering in the agent intellect and would have to possess it in a unitary manner. But this is impossible, as is clear from our lack of knowledge of many things in this world. But even were we to possess such knowledge, we would not possess it in the orderly and unified manner in which it exists in the agent intellect.

Gersonides finally turns to three objections that may be raised against his theory that the material intellect is attached in some fashion to the body and that at the same time as the acquired intellect it can become immortal through the acquisition of knowledge.[188] One such objection is that since the acquisition of any knowledge would qualify human beings for immortality, the acquisition of much knowledge would be futile. Gersonides replies that the acquisition of more knowledge is commendable, since more knowledge produces greater unity, and with it different degrees of immortality.

At this point the reader may gain the impression that Gersonides' philosophic understanding of human immortality is rather far removed from its religious meaning. Gersonides, however, assures him that

> If anyone thinks that religious faith requires a conception of human perfection [that is, immortality] different from the one we have mentioned … let him surely know that we have not assented to the view that our reason has suggested without determining its compatibility with our Torah.[189]

And he adds that should there be an incompatibility between religion and philosophy, "the incompatibility is to be attributed to our shortcomings."

Notes

[1]   Ramban (Nachmanides), *Writings and Discourses*, trans. Ch. B. Chavel (New York: Shilo, 1978), vol. 2, 12:549-51 (Hebrew: *Kitbei Rabenu Mosheh ben Nahman*, ed. Ch. B. Chavel (Jerusalem: Mosad ha-Rav Kook, 1963), 2.12:311.

[2]   For the history of messianic movements, see Marc Saperstein, ed., *Essential Papers on Messianic Movements and Personalities in Jewish History* (New York: New York University Press, 1992). See also, Harris Lenowitz, *The Jewish Messiahs: From the Galilee to Crown Heights* (Oxford: Oxford University Press, 1998); Moshe Idel, *Messianic Mystics* (Princeton:

Princeton University Press, 1998); Matt Goldish, "New Approaches to Jewish Messianism," *AJS Review*, 25, no. 1 (2000-01): 71-83; Julius H. Greenstone, *The Messiah Idea in Jewish History* (Philadelphia: Jewish Publication Society, 1906); Abba H. Silver, *A History of Messianic Speculation in Israel from the First through the Seventeenth Centuries* (New York: Macmillan, 1927); Aviezer Ravitzky, *Messianism, Zionism, and Jewish Radicalism*, trans. M. Swirsky and J. Chipman (Chicago: Chicago University Press, 1996); Craig A. Evans and Peter W. Flint, eds., *Eschatology, Messianism and the Dead Sea Scrolls* (Grand Rapids, Mich.: W. B. Eerdmans, 1997); James H. Charlesworth, ed., *The Messiah: Developments in Earliest Judaism and Christianity* (Minneapolis: Fortress, 1992). For a typology of messianic speculations, see Gershom Scholem, "Toward an Understanding of the Messianic Idea in Judaism," in *The Messianic Idea in Judaism and Other Essays on Jewish Spirituality* (New York: Schocken Books, 1995),1-36. For a general work on eschatology in antiquity, see R. H. Charles, *Eschatology: The Doctrine of a Future Life in Israel, Judaism and Christianity*, introduction by G. W. Buchanan (New York: Schocken Books, 1963).

3   Biblical citations were taken from *The Holy Scriptures according to the Masoretic Text: A New Translation* (Philadelphia: Jewish Publication Society, 1955).

4   For biblical descriptions of the Messiah, see Joseph Klausner, *The Messianic Idea in Israel, from its Beginning to the Completion of the Mishnah*, trans. W. F. Stinespring (New York: Macmillan, 1955).

5   Babylonian Talmud, Sanhedrin 97b. An English translation of the Babylonian Talmud may be found in The Babylonian Talmud, ed. I. Epstein, 35 vols. (London: Soncino Press, 1935-52). The Babylonian Talmud is cited as T.B., the name of the tractate, and the page number.

6   Josephus, *The Jewish Wars, Books I-III*, trans. H. St. J. Thackeray (Cambridge, Mass.: Harvard University Press, 1961), 2.8.11:381-82.

7   Josephus, *Jewish Wars*, 2.8.11:383.

8   Josephus, *Jewish Wars*, 2.8.14:385-87.

9   Josephus, *Jewish Wars*, 2.8.14:387.

10 Josephus, *Jewish Antiquities, Books XVIII-XX*, trans. Louis H. Feldman (Cambridge, Mass.: Harvard University Press, 1965), 18.l.3:13.

11 Josephus, *Jewish Antiquities*, 18.1.4:13.

12 Josephus, *Jewish Antiquities*, 18.1.5:15.

13 The Acts of the Apostles, in *The Complete Bible: An American Translation*, The New Testament, trans. Edgar J. Goodspeed (Chicago: University of Chicago Press, 1938), 22:23-23:10.

14 Second Book of Maccabees, in *The Complete Bible*, Apocrypha, trans. Edgar J. Goodspeed, 12:38-45.

15 Ezekiel, 38-39.

16 Ezekiel, 39:28-29.

17 For a summary of rabbinic eschatology, see George F. Moore, *Judaism in the First Centuries of the Christian Era* (Cambridge, Mass.: Harvard University Press, 1946), 2:279-395; Ephraim E. Urbach, *The Sages: Their Concepts and Beliefs* (Jerusalem: Magnes Press, 1979), 1:649-690; Leo Landman, ed., *Messianism in the Talmudic Era* (New York: Ktav Publishing House, 1979).

18 Mishnah, Sanhedrin 10.1. An English translation of the Mishnah may be found in *The Mishnah*, trans. Herbert Danby (Oxford: Oxford University Press, 1938).

19 T.B. Berakhot 17a.

20 T.B. Sanhedrin 98a.

21 T.B. Shabbat 118b.

22 T.B. Yoma 86b.

23 Jerusalem Talmud, Ta'anit 63d.

24 T.B. Abodah Zara 9a. The passage continues: "Through our many sins a number of these have already passed [and the Messiah has not yet come]."

25 T.B. Sanhedrin 97a.

26 T.B. Sanhedrin 97a.

27 Pirkei de-Rabbi Eliezer, trans. Gerald Friedlander (London, 1916; rprt. New York, Hermon Press, 1965) #43:344 (Hebrew: ed. Warsaw; rprt. New York: OM Publishing Company, 1946, #43:104).

28 T.B. Sanhedrin 98b; Shabbat 118a; Pesahim 118a.

29 *Mekilta de-Rabbi Ishmael*, Tr. Vayassaʿ, ed. and trans. Jacob Z. Lauterbach, vol. 2 (Philadelphia: Jewish Publication Society, 1933), 123.

30 *Midrash Rabbah*, Song of Songs, trans. Maurice Simon (London: Soncino Press, 1939), vol. 9, 2.13.4:126 (Hebrew: *Midrash Rabbah,* Shir ha-Shirim, ed. Shimshon Dunsky [Jerusalem: Dvir, 1980], 71).

31 *Midrash Rabbah*, Song of Songs, 2.13.1:123 (Hebrew: 69).

32 T.B. Baba Bathra 74b.

33 T.B. Sanhedrin 99a.

34 *Sifre, a Tannaitic Commentary on the Book of Deuteronomy*, trans. Reuven Hammer (New Haven: Yale University Press, 1986) Paragraph 317:324-25 (Hebrew: *Sifrei ʿal Sefer Debarim*, ed. Louis Finkelstein [New York: Jewish Theological Seminary, 1966] 360-61).

35 T.B. Ketubot 111b.

36 T.B. Berakhot 12b-13a.

37 T.B. Sukkah 52a.

38 T.B. Baba Batra 123b.

39 Henry Malter, *Saadia Gaon: His Life and Works* (Philadelphia: Jewish Publication Society, 1921; rpr. 1969). See also, Jacob Guttmann, *Die Religionsphilosophie des Saadia* (Göttingen: Vanderhoeck & Ruprecht, 1882; rprt. 1981), 194-256.

40 Cited from Saadiah Gaon, *Book of Doctrines and Beliefs*, trans. and ed. Alexander Altmann, pp. 13-14, in *Three Jewish Philosophers* (New York: Atheneum, 1985).

41 Saadiah Gaon, *The Book of Beliefs and Opinions*, trans. Samuel Rosenblatt (New Haven: Yale University Press, 1948), Introductory Treatise 2, p. 7 (Judaeo Arabic and Modern Hebrew versions: *Sefer ha-Nibhar be-Emunot u-we-Deʿot*, ed. and trans. Joseph Kafaḥ [Jerusalem: Sura, 1970], 5; Medieval Hebrew: *Sefer ha-Emunot we-Deʿot*, trans. Judah Ibn Tibbon, ed. David Slucki [Leipzig, 1864, rprt, Berlin], 3).

42 Saadiah, *Book of Beliefs*, Introductory Treatise 2, p. 7 (Judaeo Arabic and Modern Hebrew: 5-7; Medieval Hebrew: 3).

43 Saadiah, *Book of Beliefs*, Introductory Treatise 2, p. 4.

44 Saadiah, *Book of Beliefs*, 1.3. I do not give page references to complete chapters.

45 Much has been written about the origin of Kalâm and the meaning of the term, but for our purposes it is sufficient to refer to H. A. Wolfson, *The Philosophy of the Kalam* (Cambridge, Mass.: Harvard University Press, 1976), 1-111; Wolfson, *Repercussions of the Kalam in Jewish Philosophy* (Cambridge, Mass.: Harvard University Press, 1979); M. Cook, "The Origins of Kalam," *Bulletin of the School of Oriental Studies* 43 (1980): 32-43.

46 Saadiah, *Book of Beliefs,* 1-3. These are the topics of the first three treatises of the work.

47 Saadiah, *Book of Beliefs*, 4. This is the topic of the fourth treatise.

48 G. Vajda, *Introduction à la pensée juive du Moyen Age* (Paris: Vrin,1947), 48-49.

49 Saadiah, *Book of Beliefs*, 6.1-3. For a summary of Saadiah's view concerning the nature of the human soul and his eschatology, see Malter, *Saadiah Gaon*, 221-47.

50 Saadiah, *Book of Beliefs*, 6.1:236 and 1.3:55-58 (Judaeo Arabic and Modern Hebrew: 194 and 49-51; Medieval Hebrew: 95 and 24-25).

51 Saadiah, *Book of Beliefs*, 6.1:236 and 1.3:58-66 (Judaeo Arabic and Modern Hebrew: 194 and 51-58; Medieval Hebrew: 95 and 26-29).

52 Saadiah, *Book of Beliefs*, 6.3.

53 Saadiah, *Book of Beliefs*, 6.4.

54 Saadiah, *Book of Beliefs*, 6.5.

55 Saadiah, *Book of Beliefs*, 6.6. For the principle of "afflictions of love" (*yissurin shel ahabah*), see *Book of Beliefs*, 5.3.

56 Saadiah, *Book of Beliefs*, 6.7:255-56 (Judaeo Arabic and Modern Hebrew: 210-11; Medieval Hebrew: 102).

57 Saadiah, *Book of Beliefs*, 6.7:256-57 (Judaeo Arabic and Modern Hebrew: 212; Medieval Hebrew: 102).

58 Saadiah, *Book of Beliefs*, 6.7:257-58 (Judaeo Arabic and Modern Hebrew: 212-13; Medieval Hebrew: 102-03).

59 This topic is discussed in the ninth treatise of the *Book of Beliefs.*

60 Saadiah, *Book of Beliefs*, 6.8.

61 The English translation of the Oxford manuscript is found in *Book of Beliefs*, 264-89; the English translation of the

Leningrad manuscript is found in *Book of Beliefs*, 409-435. Since the English translation in the text and Kafah's edition and modern Hebrew translation are based on the Oxford manuscript, while Ibn Tibbon's translation reflects the Leningrad manuscript, I saw no need to give any reference to Ibn Tibbon's Hebrew translation.

62 Saadiah, *Book of Beliefs*, 7.1. For medieval discussions of the Messiah, see Joseph Sarachek, *The Doctrine of the Messiah in Medieval Jewish Literature* (New York: Hermon Press, 1968).

63 Saadiah, *Book of Beliefs*, 1.1.

64 Saadiah, *Book of Beliefs*, 7.2.

65 Saadiah, *Book of Beliefs*, 7.3:267-68 (Judaeo Arabic and Modern Hebrew: 221).

66 Saadiah, *Book of Beliefs*, 7.3:268-69 (Judaeo Arabic and Modern Hebrew: 221-22).

67 Saadiah, *Book of Beliefs*, 7.3:270-71 (Judaeo Arabic and Modern Hebrew: 222-23).

68 Saadiah, *Book of Beliefs*, 7.6.

69 Saadiah, *Book of Beliefs*, 7.7:277-78 (Judaeo Arabic and Modern Hebrew: 227-28).

70 Saadiah, *Book of Beliefs*, 7.7:278-80 (Judaeo Arabic and Modern Hebrew: 228-29).

71 Saadiah, *Book of Beliefs*, 7.9:286 (Judaeo Arabic and Modern Hebrew: 234).

72 Saadiah, *Book of Beliefs*, 7.9:286 (Judaeo Arabic and Modern Hebrew: 234).

73 Saadiah, *Book of Beliefs*, 7.9:286-88 (Judaeo Arabic and Modern Hebrew: 234-35).

74 Saadiah, *Book of Beliefs*, 7.9:288-89 (Judaeo Arabic and Modern Hebrew: 235-36).

75 Saadiah, *Book of Beliefs*, 8.1.

76 Saadiah, Book of Beliefs, 8.2:294-95 (Judaeo Arabic and Modern Hebrew: 241; Medieval Hebrew: 119-20).

77 Saadiah, *Book of Beliefs*, 8.3-4.

78 Saadia *Book of Beliefs*, 8.5. For Armilus, introduced rather late (seventh century C.E.) into the eschatological scheme, see David Berger, "Three Typological Themes in Early Jewish Messianism: Messiah Son of Joseph, Rabbinic Calculations,

and the Figure of Armilus," *AJS Review* 10 (1985), 141-65. For an English translation of texts dealing with Armilus, see Raphael Patai, *The Messiah Texts* (New York: Avon Books, 1979), 156-64.

79 Saadiah, *Book of Beliefs*, 8.6:304-05 (Judaeo Arabic and Modern Hebrew: 247-48; Medieval Hebrew: 123).

80 Saadiah, *Book of Beliefs*, 8.6:305-08 (Judaeo Arabic and Modern Hebrew: 248-50; Medieval Hebrew: 123-124).

81 Saadiah, *Book of Beliefs*, 8.6:309-12 (Judaeo Arabic and Modern Hebrew: 251-52; Medieval Hebrew: 125-26).

82 Saadiah, *Book of Beliefs*, 8.7. For the Rabbi Hillel who proposed this opinion, see T.B. Sanhedrin 99a.

83 Saadiah, *Book of Beliefs*, 8.8:315-16 (Judaeo Arabic and Modern Hebrew: 254-55; Medieval Hebrew: 126-27).

84 Saadiah, *Book of Beliefs*, 8.8:316-17 (Judaeo Arabic and Modern Hebrew: 255-56; Medieval Hebrew: 127).

85 Saadiah, *Book of Beliefs*, 8.8:317-19 (Judaeo Arabic and Modern Hebrew: 256-57; Medieval Hebrew: 127-28).

86 Saadiah, *Book of Beliefs*, 8.9. For Saadiah's arguments against the abrogation of the Law, see *Book of Beliefs*, 3.7-10; for his anti-trinitarian arguments, see *Book of Beliefs*, 2.5-7.

87 Saadiah, *Book of Beliefs*, 9.1:323-25 (Judaeo Arabic and Modern Hebrew: 261-62; Medieval Hebrew: 130-31).

88 Saadiah, *Book of Beliefs*, 9.1:325-26 (Judaeo Arabic and Modern Hebrew: 262-63; Medieval Hebrew: 131).

89 Saadiah, *Book of Beliefs*, 9.2:326-27 (Judaeo Arabic and Modern Hebrew: 263-64; Medieval Hebrew: 131).

90 Saadiah, *Book of Beliefs*, 9.2:327-28 (Judaeo Arabic and Modern Hebrew: 264-65; Medieval Hebrew: 131).

91 Saadiah, *Book of Beliefs*, 9.2:330 (Judaeo Arabic and Modern Hebrew: 266; Medieval Hebrew: 131).

92 Saadiah, *Book of Beliefs*, 9.4:333-34 (Judaeo Arabic and Modern Hebrew: 269; Medieval Hebrew: 133).

93 Saadiah, *Book of Beliefs*, 9.4:334 (Judaeo Arabic and Modern Hebrew: 269; Medieval Hebrew: 133-34).

94 Saadiah, *Book of Beliefs*, 9.5:336-39 (Judaeo Arabic and Modern Hebrew: 271-73; Medieval Hebrew: 134-36).

95 Saadiah, *Book of Beliefs*, 9.5:339 (Judaeo Arabic and Modern Hebrew: 273-74; Medieval Hebrew: 136).

[96] Saadiah, *Book of Beliefs*, 9.6:341-43 (Judaeo Arabic and Modern Hebrew: 275-76; Medieval Hebrew: 136-37).

[97] Saadiah, *Book of Beliefs*, 9.6:343 (Judaeo Arabic and Modern Hebrew: 276-77; Medieval Hebrew: 137).

[98] Saadiah, *Book of Beliefs*, 9.7:344-46 (Judaeo Arabic and Modern Hebrew: 277-79; Medieval Hebrew: 137-39).

[99] Saadiah, *Book of Beliefs*, 9.8.

[100] Saadiah, *Book of Beliefs*, 9.9:350-51 (Judaeo Arabic and Modern Hebrew: 282-83; Medieval Hebrew: 141).

[101] Saadiah, *Book of Beliefs*, 9.10:353-54 (Judaeo Arabic and Modern Hebrew: 283-84; Medieval Hebrew: 142).

[102] On Ibn Gabirol's philosophy, see Jacques Schlanger, *La philosophie de Salomon Ibn-Gabirol* (Leiden: Brill, 1968); Salomon Munk, *Mélanges de philosophie juive et arabe* (Paris,1857; repr.1955). Munk's work also contains Falqera's Hebrew abridgment of *Fons vitae*.

[103] Solomon Ibn Gabirol, *The Kingly Crown*, trans. Bernard Lewis (London: Valentine Mitchel, 1961) 2:28-29 (Hebrew: *Keter Malkhut*, ed. Y. A. Zeidman [Jerusalem: Mosad ha-Rav Kook, 1950], 8-10).

[104] Ibn Gabirol, *Kingly Crown*, 7-26:31-47 (Hebrew: 14-53).

[105] Ibn Gabirol, *Kingly Crown*, 27:47-48 (Hebrew: 54-56).

[106] Ibn Gabirol, *Kingly Crown*, 28:48-49 (Hebrew: 56-58).

[107] Avencebrol (Ibn Gebirol), *Fons vitae* , ed. Clemens Baeumker (Münster: Aschendorf, 1895; repr. 1995), 1.2:4.

[108] Avencebrol, *Fons vitae*, 1.2:4-7.

[109] Avencebrol, *Fons vitae*, 1.4:6.

[110] Avencebrol, *Fons vitae*, 5.38:326.

[111] Avencebrol, *Fons vitae*, 5.40:330.

[112] Avencebrol, *Fons vitae*, 5.43:338.

[113] Ibn Gabirol, *Kingly Crown*, 9:32-33 (Hebrew: 20-26).

[114] Moses Maimonides, *Commentary on the Mishnah*, Sanhedrin 10, in Isadore Twersky, *A Maimonides Reader* (New York: Behrman House, 1972), 402. The Judaeo Arabic text with a modern Hebrew translation is found in *Mishnah 'im Perush Rabenu Moshe ben Maimon*, Masekhet Sanhedrin, ed. and trans. Joseph Kafaḥ (Jerusalem: Mosad ha-Rav Kook, 1968), 195-96. The medieval Hebrew translation is conveniently found in *Haqdamot le-Ferush ha-Mishnah*, Haqdamah

le-Fereq Heleq, ed. Rabinowitz (Jerusalem: Mosad ha-Rav Kook, 1961), 109-11. For discussions of Maimonides' eschatological theories, see Jacob Dienstag, ed., *Eschatology in Maimonides' Thought: Messianism, Resurrection, and the World to Come* (New York: Ktav Publishing House, 1983).

[115] Maimonides, *Commentary on the Mishnah*, Sanhedrin 10:402-403 (Judaeo Arabic and Modern Hebrew: 196-97; Medieval Hebrew: 111-13).

[116] Maimonides, *Commentary on the Mishnah*, Sanhedrin 10: 414 (Judaeo Arabic and Modern Hebrew: 206-07; Medieval Hebrew: 129).

[117] Maimonides, *Mishneh Torah,* Book of Knowledge, ed. and trans. Moses Hyamson (Jerusalem: Boys Town, 1962), Laws of Repentance, 3.6:84b.

[118] Maimonides, *Essay on Resurrection [of the Dead]*, in *Crisis and Leadership: Epistles of Maimonides*, trans. and notes by Abraham Halkin and David Hartman (Philadelphia: Jewish Publication Society, 1985), 216-225 (Judaeo Arabic: *Iggeret (Ma'amar) Tehiyyat ha-Metim*, ed. Yishaq Shailat [Jerusalem: Ma'aliyot, 1987] 1: 324-32; Hebrew: *Iggeret (Ma'amar) Tehiyyat ha-Metim*, ed. Shailat, 1:348-64). For the controversy about Maimonides' belief in the resurrection of the dead and his eschatology, see Daniel J. Silver, *Maimonidean Criticism and the Maimonidean Controversy 1180-1240* (Leiden: Brill, 1965), index under "resurrection," "*Olam ha-Ba*," and "Messiah and Messianic Age."

[119] Maimonides, *Commentary on the Mishnah*, Sanhedrin 10:414-16 (Judaeo Arabic and Modern Hebrew: 207-08; Medieval Hebrew: 129-32).

[120] Maimonides, *Commentary on the Mishnah*, Sanhedrin 10:413-14 (Judaeo Arabic and Modern Hebrew: 206; Medieval Hebrew: 128-29).

[121] Maimonides, *Mishneh Torah*, Book of Kings and Wars, 12.11-12, and appendix from the uncensored edition, in Twersky, *Maimonides Reader*, 222-27. For the Hebrew text, see *Mishneh Torah*, Hilkhot Melakhim, ed. S. T. Rubinstein (Jerusalem: Mosad Harav Kook, 1962), 415-17.

[122] Maimonides, *Mishneh Torah*, Book of Kings and Wars, 12.11, p. 222.

[123] Maimonides, *Mishneh Torah*, Book of Kings and Wars, 12.12, p. 224.

[124] Maimonides, *Essay on Resurrection*, in *Crisis and Leadership*, 218 (Judaeo Arabic: 325; Hebrew: 351).

[125] Alexander Altmann, "Maimonides on the Intellect and Metaphysics," *Von der mittelalterlichen zur modernen Aufklärung* (Tübingen: Mohr, 1987), 60-91.

[126] Maimonides, *Guide of the Perplexed*, trans. Shlomo Pines (Chicago: University of Chicago Press, 1963) 1.70:173-74 (Pines translates "preparedness") (Arabic: *Dalâlat al-Ḥâ'irîn*, ed. I. Joel [Jerusalem: J. Junovitch, 1930-31], 119-20; Medieval Hebrew: *Moreh Nebukhim*, trans. Samuel Ibn Tibbon, ed. Eben Shemu'el [Jerusalem: Mosed ha-Rav Kook, 1981], 149-50]). For an interpretation of the meaning of this notion in Maimonides, see Altmann, "Maimonides on the Intellect," 65-71.

[127] Maimonides, *Commentary on the Mishnah*, Eight Chapters, 2:365 (Judaeo Arabic and Modern Hebrew: 376-77; Medieval Hebrew: *Haqdamot*, ed. Rabinowitz, 163-65); *Guide*, 1.72:193 (Arabic: 134; Medieval Hebrew: 167-68).

[128] For example in Maimonides, *Guide*, 1.68.

[129] Maimonides, *Guide*, 1.41:91 (Arabic: 61; Hebrew: 77).

[130] Maimonides, *Guide*, 3.27:511-12 (Arabic: 372-73; Hebrew: 370-71).

[131] Maimonides, *Guide*, 1.74 (7):221 (Arabic: 155; Hebrew: 193).

[132] Maimonides, *Guide*, Translator's Introduction, ciii-iv.

[133] Altmann, "Maimonides on the Intellect," 89-90.

[134] Maimonides, *Guide*, 2:27:333 (Arabic: 232-33; Hebrew: 290-91).

[135] Maimonides, *Commentary on the Mishnah*, Sanhedrin, 10:413 (Judaeo Arabic and Modern Hebrew: 206; Medieval Hebrew: 128-29).

[136] Maimonides, *Commentary on the Mishnah*, Sanhedrin, 10:413-14 (Judaeo Arabic and Modern Hebrew: 206; Medieval Hebrew: 129).

[137] Maimonides, *Commentary on the Mishnah*, Sanhedrin, 10:411-12 (Judaeo Arabic and Modern Hebrew: 204-05; Medieval Hebrew: 125-26).

[138] Naḥmanides, *Gate of Reward*, in *Writings*, 2.7:473-74 (Hebrew: 283). For the complexity of Naḥmanides' intellectual make-up, see David Berger, "Miracles and the Natural Order in Naḥmanides," *Rabbi Moses Naḥmanides (Ramban): Explorations in His Religious and Literary Virtuosity*, ed. Isadore Twersky (Cambridge, Mass.: Harvard University Press, 1983), 107-28.

[139] Naḥmanides, *Gate of Reward*, in *Writings*, 2.7:475 (Hebrew: 283).

[140] Naḥmanides, *Gate of Reward*, in *Writings*, 2.7:476 (Hebrew: 283).

[141] Naḥmanides, *Gates of Reward*, in *Writings*, 2.7:480 (Hebrew: 285).

[142] Naḥmanides, *Gates of Reward*, in *Writings*, 2.7:483-86 (Hebrew: 287-88).

[143] Naḥmanides, *Gates of Reward*, in *Writings*, 2.7: 486-91 (Hebrew: 288).

[144] Naḥmanides, *Gates of Reward*, in *Writings*, 2.7:491-95 (Hebrew: 290-91).

[145] Naḥmanides, *Gates of Reward*, in *Writings*, 2.8:495-97 (Hebrew: 291-92).

[146] Naḥmanides, *Gates of Reward*, in *Writings*, 2.8:497-98 (Hebrew: 292).

[147] Naḥmanides, *Gates of Reward*, in *Writings*, 2.9:498-504 (Hebrew: 292-94).

[148] Naḥmanides, *Gates of Reward*, in *Writings*, 2.9:504-07 (Hebrew: 294-95).

[149] Naḥmanides, *Gates of Reward*, in *Writings*, 2.9:507-09 (Hebrew: 295-96).

[150] Naḥmanides, *Gates of Reward*, in *Writings*, 2.9:509-12 (Hebrew: 296-97).

[151] Naḥmanides, *Gates of Reward*, in *Writings*, 2.9:509 (Hebrew: 296).

[152] Naḥmanides, *Gates of Reward*, in *Writings*, 2.9: 509-10 (Hebrew: 296).

[153] Naḥmanides, *Gates of Reward*, in *Writings*, 2.9:512 (Hebrew: 297).

[154] Naḥmanides, *Gates of Reward*, in *Writing*, 2.9:514-18 (Hebrew: 298-99).

[155] Nahmanides, *Gates of Reward*, in *Writings*, 2.10:518-32 (Hebrew: 299-304).

[156] Nahmanides, *Gates of Reward*, in *Writings*, 2.10:527 (Hebrew: 302).

[157] Nahmanides, *Gates of Reward*, in *Writings*, 2.10: 531-32 (Hebrew: 303-04).

[158] Nahmanides, *Gates of Reward*, in *Writings*, 2.10:532-33 (Hebrew: 304).

[159] Nahmanides, *Gates of Reward*, in *Writings*, 2.10:533-35 (Hebrew: 304-05).

[160] Nahmanides, *Gates of Reward*, in *Writings*, 2.10:536-37 (Hebrew: 305-06).

[161] Nahmanides, *Gates of Reward*, in *Writings*, 2.10:537 (Hebrew: 306).

[162] Nahmanides, *Gates of Reward*, in *Writings*, 2.10:538 (Hebrew: 306).

[163] Nahmanides, *Gates of Reward*, in *Writings*, 2.10:541-43 (Hebrew: 307-08).

[164] Nahmanides, *Gates of Reward*, in *Writings*, 2.10:543-49 (Hebrew: 308-11).

[165] Levi ben Gershom (Gersonides), *The Wars of the Lord: Book 1, Immortality of the Soul*, trans. with an introduction and notes by Seymour Feldman (Philadelphia: Jewish Publication Society, 1984), Introductory Remarks, 92-93 (Hebrew: *Sefer Milhamot Hashem* [Leipzig: Carl Lorck, 1866; rprt. Berlin: Louis Lamm, 1923). For corrections to the Hebrew text, see *The Wars of the Lord*, trans. Seymour Feldman, 227-41.

[166] Gersonides, *Wars*, Introductory Remarks, 101 (Hebrew: 8).

[167] Harry A. Wolfson, "Plan for the Publication of a *Corpus Commentariorum Averrois in Aristotelem*," *Speculum* 6 (1931), 412-27, revised in *Speculum* 38 (1963), 88-104; rprt. in *Studies in the History of Philosophy and Religion* (Cambridge, Mass.: Harvard University Press, 1973) 1:430-55.

[168] Aristotle, *De anima* 3.5.

[169] Aristotle, *De anima* 3.7.

[170] Aristotle, *De anima* 3.5.

[171] Gersonides, *Wars*, 1.1:109-10 (Hebrew: 12-13). For a discussion of Gersonides' theory of the human intellect and

immortality, see Charles Touati, *La pensée philosophique et théologique de Gersonide* (Paris: Les Éditions de Minuit, 1973), 395-442. See also, Alfred L. Ivry, "Gersonides and Averroes on the Intellect: The Evidence of the Supercommentary on the *De Anima*," in *Gersonide en son temps*, ed. Gilbert Dahan (Louvain-Paris: E. Peeters, 1991), 235-51, and Herbert A. Davidson, "Gersonides on the Material and Active Intellects," in *Studies on Gersonides: A Fourteenth Century Jewish Philosopher-Scientist*, ed. Gad Freudenthal (Leiden: Brill, 1992), 195-265.

[172] Gersonides, *Wars*, 1.2:111-19 (Hebrew: 13-19).

[173] Gersonides, *Wars*, 1.3:120-29 (Hebrew: 19-25).

[174] Gersonides, *Wars*, 1.4:130-43 (Hebrew: 25-35).

[175] Gersonides, *Wars*, 1.5:144-45 (Hebrew: 35-36).

[176] Gersonides, *Wars*, 1.6:146-47 (Hebrew: 36-37).

[177] Gersonides, *Wars*, 1.6:147-48 (Hebrew: 38).

[178] Gersonides, *Wars*, 1.6:148-50 (Hebrew: 38-39).

[179] Gersonides, *Wars*, 1.6:160-64 (Hebrew: 45-48).

[180] Gersonides, *Wars*, 1.7:165-69 (Hebrew: 48-51).

[181] Gersonides, *Wars*, 1.8:170-71 (Hebrew: 51-52).

[182] Gersonides, *Wars*, 1.8:170 (Hebrew: 51-52).

[183] Gersonides, *Wars*, 1.8:171 (Hebrew: 52).

[184] Gersonides, *Wars*, 1.9-10.

[185] Gersonides, *Wars*, 1.11:212-17 (Hebrew: 81-85).

[186] Gersonides, *Wars*, 1.11:212 (Hebrew: 81).

[187] Gersonides, *Wars*, 1.12:218-22 (Hebrew: 85-88).

[188] Gersonides, *Wars*, 1.13. 223-25 (Hebrew: 89-91).

[189] Gersonides, *Wars*, 1.14:226 (Hebrew: 91).

The Aquinas Lectures

19. *Realism And Nominalism Revisited.* Henry Veatch (1954)
ISBN 0-87462-119-4

20. *Imprudence in St. Thomas Aquinas.* Charles J. O'Neil (1955)
ISBN 0-87462-120-8

21. *The Truth That Frees.* Gerard Smith, S.J. (1956)
ISBN 0-87462-121-6

22. *St. Thomas and the Future of Metaphysics.* Joseph Owens,
C.Ss.R. (1957) ISBN 0-87462-122-4

23. *Thomas and the Physics of 1958: A Confrontation.* Henry
Margenau (1958) ISBN 0-87462-123-2

24. *Metaphysics and Ideology.* Wm. Oliver Martin (1959)
ISBN 0-87462-124-0

25. *Language, Truth and Poetry.* Victor M. Hamm (1960)
ISBN 0-87462-125-9

26. *Metaphysics and Historicity.* Emil L. Fackenheim (1961)
ISBN 0-87462-126-7

27. *The Lure of Wisdom.* James D. Collins (1962)
ISBN 0-87462-127-5

28. *Religion and Art.* Paul Weiss (1963) ISBN 0-87462-128-3

29. *St. Thomas and Philosophy.* Anton C. Pegis (1964)
ISBN 0-87462-129-1

30. *The University in Process.* John O. Riedl (1965)
ISBN 0-87462-130-5

31. *The Pragmatic Meaning of God.* Robert O. Johann (1966)
ISBN 0-87462-131-3

32. *Religion and Empiricism.* John E. Smith (1967)
ISBN 0-87462-132-1

33. *The Subject.* Bernard Lonergan, S.J. (1968)
ISBN 0-87462-133-X

34. *Beyond Trinity.* Bernard J. Cooke (1969)
ISBN 0-87462-134-8

35. *Ideas and Concepts.* Julius R. Weinberg (1970)
ISBN 0-87462-135-6

36. *Reason and Faith Revisited.* Francis H. Parker (1971)
ISBN 0-87462-136-4

37. *Psyche and Cerebrum.* John N. Findlay (1972)
ISBN 0-87462-137-2

38. *The Problem of the Criterion.* Roderick M. Chisholm (1973)
ISBN 0-87462-138-0

39. *Man as Infinite Spirit.* James H. Robb (1974)
ISBN 0-87462-139-9

40. *Aquinas to Whitehead: Seven Centuries of Metaphysics of Religion.* Charles Hartshorne (1976) ISBN 0-87462-141-0

41. *The Problem of Evil.* Errol E. Harris (1977)
ISBN 0-87462-142-9

42. *The Catholic University and the Faith.* Francis C. Wade, S.J. (1978) ISBN 0-87462-143-7

43. *St. Thomas and Historicity.* Armand J. Maurer, C.S.B. (1979) ISBN 0-87462-144-5

44. *Does God Have a Nature?* Alvin Plantinga (1980)
ISBN 0-87462-145-3

45. *Rhyme and Reason: St. Thomas and Modes of Discourse.* Ralph Mcinerny (1981) ISBN 0-87462-148-8

46. *The Gift: Creation.* Kenneth L. Schmitz (1982)
ISBN 0-87462-149-6

47. *How Philosophy Begins.* Beatrice H. Zedler (1983)
ISBN 0-87462-151-8

48. *The Reality of the Historical Past.* Paul Ricoeur (1984)
ISBN 0-87462-152-6

49. *Human Ends and Human Actions: An Exploration in St. Thomas' Treatment.* Alan Donagan (1985) ISBN 0-87462-153-4

50. *Imagination and Metaphysics in St. Augustine.* Robert O'Connell, S.J. (1986) ISBN 0-87462-227-1

51. *Expectations of Immortality in Late Antiquity.* Hilary A Armstrong (1987) ISBN 0-87462-154-2

52. *The Self.* Anthony Kenny (1988) ISBN 0-87462-155-0

53. *The Nature of Philosophical Inquiry.*Quentin Lauer, S.J. (1989) ISBN 0-87562-156-9

54. *First Principles, Final Ends and Contemporary Philosophical Issues.* Alasdair MacIntyre (1990) ISBN 0-87462-157-7

55. *Descartes among the Scholastics.* Marjorie Greene (1991)
ISBN 0-87462-158-5

56. *The Inference That Makes Science.*Ernan McMullin (1992)
ISBN 0-87462-159-3

57. *Person and Being.* W. Norris Clarke, S.J. (1993)
ISBN 0-87462-160-7

58. *Metaphysics and Culture.* Louis Dupré (1994) ISBN 0-87462-161-5

59. *Mediæval Reactions to the Encounters between Faith and Reason.* John F. Wippel (1995) ISBN 0-87462-162-3

60. *Paradoxes of Time in Saint Augustine.* Roland J. Teske, S.J. (1996) ISBN 0-87462-163-1

61. *Simplicity As Evidence of Truth.* Richard Swinburne (1997) ISBN 0-87462-164-X

62. *Science, Religion and Authority: Lessons from the Galileo Affair.* Richard J. Blackwell. (1998) ISBN 0-87462-165-8

63. *What Sort of Human Nature? Medieval Philosophy and the Systematics of Christology.* Marilyn McCord Adams. (1999) ISBN 0-87462-166-6

64. *On Inoculating Moral Philosophy against God.* John M. Rist. (2000) ISBN 0-87462-167-X.

65. *A Sensible Metaphysical Realism.* William P. Alston (2001) ISBN 0-87462-168-2.

66. *Eschatological Themes in Medieval Jewish Philosophy.* Arthur Hyman (2002) ISBN 0-87462-169-0.

ISBN 0-87462-169-0

51500

9 780874 621693

About the Aquinas Lecture Series

The Annual St. Thomas Aquinas Lecture Series began at Marquette University in the Spring of 1937. Ideal for classroom use, library additions, or private collections, the Aquinas Lecture Series has received international acceptance by scholars, universities, and libraries. Hardbound in maroon cloth with gold stamped covers. Uniform style and price ($15 each). Some reprints with soft covers. Complete set (64 Titles) (ISBN 0-87462-150-X) receives a 40% discount. New standing orders receive a 30% discount. Regular reprinting keeps all volumes available. Ordering information (purchase orders, checks, and major credit cards accepted):

Marquette University Press
30 Amberwood Parkway
P.O. Box 2139
Ashland OH 44805
    Order Toll-Free (800) 247-6553
    FAX: (419) 281 6883

Editorial Address:
    Dr. Andrew Tallon, Director
    Marquette University Press
    Box 3141
    Milwaukee WI 53201-3141
    Tel: (414) 288-7298 FAX: (414) 288-7813
    email: andrew.tallon@marquette.edu.

http://www.mu.edu/mupress/